American Serfdom

vs. eternal vigilance is the price of liberty

Jefferson Told Us:

"If the American People ever allow the banks to control the issuance of their currency, first by inflation and then by deflation, the banks and corporations that will grow up around them will deprive the people of all their property, until their children will wake up homeless on the continent their fathers occupied. The issuing of money should be taken from the banks and restored to Congress and the people to whom it belongs." –Thomas Jefferson

Order this book online at www.trafford.com
or email orders@trafford.com

Most Trafford titles are also available at major online book retailers.

Note for Librarians: A cataloguing record for this book is available from Library
and Archives Canada at www.collectionscanada.ca/amicus/index-e.html

Printed in Victoria, BC, Canada.

ISBN: 978-1-4269-1603-8 (sc)

*Our mission is to efficiently provide the world's finest, most comprehensive book publishing
service, enabling every author to experience success. To find out how to publish your
book, your way, and have it available worldwide, visit us online at www.trafford.com*

Trafford rev. 8/24/2009

 www.trafford.com

North America & international
toll-free: 1 888 232 4444 (USA & Canada)
phone: 250 383 6864 ♦ fax: 812 355 4082

Contents

Basing your life on lies despite evidence does not make you a well-balanced person, may be sincere but is submission to untruthfulness, and will lead to disaster. —Bridger Daquan

Eternal Vigilance is the Price of Liberty, not faith or hope

Chapter I

Introduction

My dad told me many times that my mother's grandfather was known as the infidel of the high plains.

My mother told me many times that once in a while when she and some family members got the courage to go to a local church, the preacher would scare her to death preaching that her father and grandfather would burn for all eternity in hellfire and brimstone.

In spite of this, my mother had a longing to join a church [I guess this was due to peer pressure] and finally decided to join the Christian Science Church and later became a practitioner.

One thing I distinctly remember about my attendance of the Christian Science Church was every time I attended this church, the first reader would read from the *Christian Science Book of Science and Health With Key to the Scriptures by Mary Baker Eddie* the words "***Spirit is real and eternal. Matter is unreal and temporal.***"

From the time I was ten years of age, my mother told me over and over that I should be an engineer. So, I set my sights at becoming an engineer. In the pursuit of becoming an engineer I took high school physics.

I was very fortunate to have an excellent high school physics teacher. On page 7 of my high school physics book, it said "**Matter is indestructible.** If we weigh a block of ice, melt it, and weigh the water, which is formed, we find that there is no change in weight. *No matter has been lost.* The chemist may let a piece of iron rust, and then recover the iron from the rust. It will have the same weight as the original piece of iron. We may change the form of matter or change its state, but we cannot destroy it. While we cannot destroy matter by means of either a physical or chemical change, neither can we create matter. Hence the total quantity of matter in the universe is the same today as yesterday. The fact that matter cannot be created or destroyed is usually called the *law of conservation of matter.*"

Somehow I knew to the core of my being that here was a book that actually told the truth! Truth, I deeply love! This would ultimately change my life.

It clearly dawned on me that this law was in direct conflict with what I was [and had been] hearing at church! I needed to find out what was the truth?

What was the basis of each of the two conflicting descriptions of the world we live in?

From that point on in my life, I began noticing that science and religion tell a completely different story about how the universe works, how it came about, and how it is.

I was, from the time I took high school physics;

always intrigued by the idea that *matter could not be created or destroyed.*

I was also intrigued with the idea that *energy could not be created or destroyed.*

The *material balance* expressed in chemical equations wherein the number and kind of atoms on one side of the equation always equaled the number and kind of atoms on the other side of the equation especially intrigued me.

You could burn a house down, but the number and kind of atoms involved in the chemical reaction[s] of burning down the house before the fire always equals the number and kind of atoms still existing after the fire.

To me this meant that fundamental constituents are eternal, i.e., cannot be created or destroyed.

I always wondered if my essence (and every living creature's essence) was a fundamental constituent that was eternal.

I have subjectively observed that I have a consciousness [I'm not talking about conscience] that is only suspended while I sleep and at all other periods of time seems constant from the time I was first aware of it in my childhood until now, and it seems independent of knowledge, belief system, conscience, pain or pleasure.

It also seems that it has always been in existence though suspended for intervals of time such as while I sleep.

It is comforting to me to believe that one of those eternal fundamental constituents is my consciousness that has been in the universe for an eternity before I was born and will be in the universe for an eternity after I die.

I hope this is true, but do not know it is true. I know this is an imaginary model of the way the world is, but I believe it is within the realm of the scientifically feasible.

I never could buy the Christian imaginary model that is not at all within the realm of the scientifically feasible, i.e., the concept that a mere Christian belief system makes a person eternal.

This additionally was and is suspect to me because it looked (and still looks) to me like a tyrant's effort to gain control of other people's belief system to thereby rule their life.

People are not born with belief systems. Each human goes from no belief system to a full-blown belief system of how the universe (or world) really is, and this belief system can change completely or be refined several times throughout each human's life.

Further, some people become brain dead, acquire Alzheimer's, become mentally ill or the like and therefore have no belief system during the latter years of their life. (But, these people still have a constant consciousness that is intermittently suspended at intervals and is independent of their belief system, conscience, pain, pleasure, worldliness etc.)

The very fact that the belief system changes proves that it is not eternal. I then believed the so-called Christian "born again" rebirth is nothing except the birth of one's Christian belief system.

But, the tyrants who want you to believe that your belief system determines whether or not you have eternal life know that if they control your belief system they control you.

I have long thought tyrannical minds had to be behind Christianity and other religions.

Later in this book we prove, at least in my mind, that this is true. Roman tyrants were behind the use of Christianity to achieve the function of tyranny.

According to the Bible the Christian "God," i.e., tyranny, is extremely jealous and bigoted and always wants you to murder anyone who does not have the particular belief system the Christian "God,"i.e., tyranny, demands.

This made (and still makes) Christianity suspect to me. The Muslim religion appears to be even worse and was and is suspect for virtually the same reasons.

Also, in my early years of pursuing an engineering degree my technical writing teacher stealthily taught our class about evolution, for which I was extremely grateful, and I was made aware that science and religion tell a completely different story about how life on earth came about and later I became aware that science and religion conflict on just about everything else.

In my early years in college I came across the words of the Declaration of Independence.

I was extremely overcome by the words "***We hold these truths to be self evident, that all men are created equal, that they are endowed by their creator with certain***

**unalienable rights, that among these rights are life, liberty
and the pursuit of happiness…"**

This was a totally different concept from Christian
dogma or Calvinism.

It embodied (and still embodies) at its core the belief
that men are born good to the core and deserve "unalienable
rights," whereas Christian dogma and Calvinism held (and
still holds) that humans are born evil sinners, so evil they can
only be saved from their evilness by the **grace of God**, i.e.,
tyranny.

From that point on I began noticing that Christian
dogma and the Bible are in conflict with the Declaration of
Independence, the Constitution, the Bill of Rights, and the
principles of the Enlightenment.

I further noticed that Christians have long been
working, for many decades, to convince the American public
that Christian dogma and the Bible are the very basis of these
documents and the United States itself.

I later noticed that people, especially religious people,
were trying to convince everyone that there is no conflict
between religion and science.

They were saying that science and religion ask
different questions and have no conflicts, i.e., science asks
how while religion asks why.

In my view this was [and is] ridiculous.

Science and religion asked (and still ask) the same
questions:

1. How the universe (or world) really is?
2. How it all came about?
3. What are the important natural phenomena (or universe characteristics) to pay heed to in the universe?

Science and Christianity (and probably all religions) found (and find) completely different answers to these questions.

I noticed that the scientific explanation for why a particular hypothesis, theory or law was [and is] so was [and is] always based on observed *evidence*.

All my investigating has found that science is based on *evidence*.

From *evidence* scientific hypothesis, theories and laws are formulated and repeatably verified.

I also noticed that a scientific theory, such as gravitational theory, was [and is] irrefutable and if one tried to defy it, it could mean that person's death.

When I asked a Christian why something was so, the answer was always "the Bible tells me so or some church authority tells me so."

They would often cite chapter and verse of the Bible or cite church dogma. Religion is based on *authority*.

The Christian and Muslim religions appeared to me to be based on first century ***authoritarianism***.

In the case of Christianity it appeared to me to be based on the first century Bible [I later found the Bible was actually put together in 325 AD].

I also noticed that the ***Christian axioms***, unlike science, are ***unverifiable from*** observable ***evidence***.

My investigation has found that the Bible has been translated multiple times and many of the original writings have been changed, left completely out or altered.

Jesus, himself, never wrote a word. ***Jesus never wrote a word.***

I understand that Gary Bauer, president of "American Values," and once a candidate for U.S. president, decided the King James Version of the Bible was written by homosexuals and caused a completely different Bible to be written.

This is the Bible my now existing oldest four children think "is the only true word of God."

It seemed (and still seems) to me that the Bible is either literally true or it is not true at all.

I knew (and still know) that the Bible is not literally true, because it makes many totally false statements; therefore, it was (and still is) not true.

It has always been amazing to me how Christians could see that the religion of Native Americans was fanciful and superstitious, but they couldn't see that their own religion was fanciful and superstitious.

Also, they could see that the Native Hawaiian religion

was fanciful and superstitious but not their own.

The same can be said of the Muslim religion etc. Also, Muslims can see that the Christian religion is fanciful and superstitious but they can't see that their own religion is fanciful and superstitious.

Actually, in other religions such as the Muslim, Native American, and Native Hawaiian religions, all Christians are atheists or the equivalent in the various other religions.

So, people of other religions, in fact, consider Christians, atheists that are evil and hell bound or the equivalent in the various other religions.

The Greeks had enough sense to realize that their belief in Zeus etc. was ridiculous and they completely overcame their belief in the Zeus belief system.

Why can't Americans be smart enough to realize how ridiculous their Christian belief system is and overcome it?

While still in high school and college, it seemed to me that virtually everyone claimed to be a Christian where I lived and if you didn't claim to be one, you were looked upon with considerable disfavor.

Popular movie stars, such as John Wayne, sent the same message.

The peer pressure, including that of women who interested me, very powerfully urged me to "become a Christian" and join a "Christian Church."

Inevitably, while I was in college I found myself in my own car with two very friendly, persuasive and charismatic Christian proselytizers talking to air filled space that was supposed to be God that I couldn't see, hear, smell, taste, feel, and could only imagine.

This process of talking to space that was supposed to be this invisible, inaudible, odorless, tasteless, untouchable, and imaginary God was saving my invisible, silent, odorless, tasteless, untouchable and imaginary soul and giving me rebirth into this invisible, silent, tasteless, odorless, untouchable and imaginary eternal life into this invisible, silent, odorless, tasteless, untouchable, and imaginary heaven.

It all seemed like a hoax to me but I temporarily went alone with it due to the very powerful peer pressure.

I later found myself in the physical structure of a church with the preacher talking to air filled space that was supposed to be this invisible, silent, odorless, tasteless, untouchable, and imaginary God that magically saved my invisible, silent, odorless, tasteless, untouchable and imaginary soul and gave me this invisible, silent, odorless, tasteless, untouchable and imaginary eternal life in this invisible, silent, odorless, tasteless, untouchable, and imaginary heaven that magically is supposed to exist.

But in the long run, I couldn't take the proselytizers or their fantasy world.

Their fantasy world was just too much for me.

It just didn't square with my knowledge of science and the realities of the real, natural, world that I was clearly living in and could vividly observe, i.e., see, hear, smell, taste and feel.

So, when it became time for me to marry, my wife, who grew up Catholic and desirous of church life, and I agreed to be married in an Episcopal Church and decided to join this church that I thought was a moderate church that actually tried, at least, to accommodate irrefutable scientific facts.

In this church, they didn't strictly interpret the insane passages in the Bible and I thought I could tolerate being a member of such a moderate church.

I had also noticed that although Jefferson did not embrace the Christian dogma he grew up in and remained a member of the Episcopal Church throughout his life.

In the mean time for a while I strived hard to be a true believer of all the imaginary Christian axioms.

I also noticed that in the Christian dogma and the Bible, I could find nothing like the principles of the Declaration of Independence, Constitution, Bill of Rights, inalienable rights, democracy, a republic or a social contract.

The source of these concepts seemed to be the Enlightenment, Greek and Roman philosophies.

The more I looked at the Bible it became clearer and clearer that it was literally about kingdoms, dictators, slavery, kings and other men who owned multiple wives plus multiple concubines, women as men's property, murdering a man's wife if she wasn't a virgin on the wedding night, murdering a woman if she was a victim of rape, killing children if they talked back to you, recitations of a four cornered flat earth adjacent the sea that was the center of the universe, a cosmos that was only six thousand years old, and the like.

While raising my children I tried very hard to impress them with how great the U.S. founding fathers were, especially Jefferson, and how great the enlightenment of people like John Locke was.

But, I began to notice that my oldest four children were completely taken over by the fundamentalist Christian view of the world and really didn't care about the principles of the Declaration of Independence, Constitution, Bill of Rights or keeping America the way the founders intended it to be.

They seemed to have somehow compartmentalized their view of the world into compartmentalized paradigms with the religion paradigm being their important real eternal life and the natural world paradigm being their unimportant and insignificant temporary life.

I felt totally blindsided. How could this have happened?

I noticed it quick enough to try my best to convince my youngest son not to be taken in by such fundamentalism, or maybe he was just smart enough not to, but I didn't realize what was happening to the others until it was too late.

This made it clear to me that part of the Christian proselytizing technique is to bigot, i.e., close people's, such as, my children's minds, completely to all reason that could cast doubt on people's, such as, my children's belief system, otherwise the proselytizer had convinced them that disbelief will condemn them and their children to hell for eternity.

Then I started noticing that fundamentalist Christians are having a very high influence over the United States.

They are destroying our schools by causing them to disseminate misinformation and ignorance.

They are destroying the sacred separation of church and state. They are destroying the meaning of the Declaration of Independence.

They are destroying the meaning of the Constitution.

They are destroying the meaning of the Bill of Rights.

They are destroying the proper functioning of the legislative, executive and judicial branches of our government.

They are destroying America.

They are unconstitutionally teaching ***creationism* in our schools**.

America is becoming one of the most scientifically and technologically ignorant countries in the world.

America was once the freethinking, science loving, and invention center of the world, but is now becoming the most bigoted, closed minded and ignorant country of the world.

I thought something has to be done.

Along about this time I took the "Belief-O-Matic" test on beliefnet.com, which showed me to be 100% Mainline to Liberal Christian Protestant. [Now it shows me to be 100% Secular Humanist].

This shocked me, but it made me realize that there are a lot of liberal Christians out there that, in truth, think a lot like I do.

The following argument I am presenting is hopefully for everyone because we all must wake up but more likely for moderate to liberal Christians as well as naturalist, atheist, agnostics, secularists, Unitarian Universalist, secular humanists, humanists, scientists, evolutionists, engineers and the like.

I also finally realized that liberal and moderate Christians like I used to be are, in fact, ***enabling*** the insane fundamentalists to destroy the United States.

I also finally learned the primary beneficiaries of the slavery Christianity has prepared Americans to live under and that is one of the things this book is about.

I now sympathize with and feel that "liberal Christians, secular humanists etc." like myself, as I used to be and now am, are in a plight similar to but worse than Thomas Jefferson's plight of living in a world of legalized slavery that he knew was wrong but could not seem to be able to stop although he tried and tried.

In the end his creditors owned his slaves and he didn't even have the power to free his own slaves.

This brilliant genius was in this terrible state of

indebtedness to his creditors primarily because he had spent his life in uncompensated or poorly compensated activities and positions because these activities and positions enabled him to do work so great that it ***gave us the greatest way of life ever to exist on this earth!***

Now, the Christians (whose Bible and Gospels actually support slavery, torture, murdering non-believers, and many other things Jefferson was fighting against) are destroying this greatest way of life ever to exist on earth!

We must stop these Christians! And the terrible results they are enabling and bringing about! The following is my attempt to do something about what I think is terribly wrong in the United States today.

A lie cannot be made true by believing or having faith that it is true, nor by prayer, nor by indoctrinating children from birth until death with the lie, nor by torturing, murdering, condemning unbelievers as blasphemers or otherwise penalizing unbelievers, nor by brilliantly marketing the lie as the truth, nor by saying only the devil could make one question the lie, nor by the fact that billions of people believe the lie. —Bridger Daquan

Chapter II

Fundamental Training Institutions And People Purposely Teaching Faithful Belief in Lies Despite Evidence

United States Constitutional reference: **Article VI**

The Senators and Representatives before mentioned, and the members of the several state legislatures, and all executive and judicial officers, both of the United States and the several states, shall be bound by oath or affiliation, to support this Constitution; *but no religious test shall ever be required as a qualification to any office or public trust under the United States*. [Bold face and italics added]

Even though the Constitution explicitly states that no religious test shall ever be required, the ignorant [of truth] and superstitious electorate [aided and abetted by the ignorant (of truth) and superstitious press of the United States] by and large *unconstitutionally* requires each "office or public trust" to be *unconstitutionally* filled with a completely conned member of the ubiquitous [Christian] Con-Artist Industry of the United States before they will vote for them.

According to Webster's New Collegiate Dictionary, Copyright 1976, slavery can be defined as "submission to a dominant influence." Also, a slave can be defined as "a person who has lost control of himself and is dominated by something or someone."

Liberty can be defined as " freedom from arbitrary or despotic control." Or also as "the positive enjoyment of various social, political, or economic rights and privileges." Freedom can be defined as "liberation from slavery or restraint or from the power of another." If you are a Christian you have undergone "submission to a dominant influence," and you have "lost control" of yourself; so, you are, by the dictionary definition of a slave, a slave. You may say, "What's the problem? This is what makes me happy." The problem is that you lay yourself and the United States open to control by evil human beings who don't care about you or the welfare of the United States.

It is revealing that Robert G. Ingersoll, 1833-1899, said:

"Religion can never reform mankind because religion is slavery."

In today's America, under these definitions, the vast majority of Americans are, by the dictionary definition, social and economic slaves even though many of them have an abundance of wonderful real world things, i.e., automobiles, television sets, computers etc. enabled by past technological advances [inventions].

It should be noted that in the days of the Gatlin Gun it cost only $4.00 to file for a U.S. Patent. This bought the right to an unlimited amount of both independent and dependent claims and an unlimited amount of figures, drawings and pages in the specification, the Patent Office search, examination, plus all amendments etc. that are required. In the 1960s it cost $30.00 for all these features one wanted or needed.

Today in 2009, it cost much more than that and there are multiple complex charges in multiple ways, i.e., a high filing fee, plus a high fee for the search, plus a high fee for the examination, plus a high fee for over a small number of claims, plus high fees on and on. So, it will be a miracle if inventions of the order turned out before Franklin Roosevelt's presidency will ever exist again.

Did the vast majority of Americans always live under the conditions of social and economic slavery? If not, when and how did this condition start taking place? Let us first examine how social slavery became the reality of life for the vast majority of Americans.

The Declaration of Independence [principally written by Thomas Jefferson, the greatest democratic visionary and friend America ever had] states:

" WE hold these Truths to be self-evident, that all Men are created equal, that they are endowed by their Creator with certain unalienable Rights, that among these are Life, Liberty, and the Pursuit of Happiness—That to secure these Rights, Governments are instituted among Men, deriving their just Powers from the Consent of the Governed, that whenever any Form of Government becomes destructive to these Ends, it is the Right of

*the People to alter or to abolish it, and to institute new
Government, laying its Foundation on such Principles, and
organizing its Powers in such Form, as to them shall seem
most likely to effect their Safety and Happiness."*

This is what was written to motivate the loss of
American's lives in the American Revolution. So, under
the Jeffersonian America, Americans [except for blacks]
intellectually had both social and economic liberty and
freedom. He, especially, went to great lengths to make
certain this was so.

But, is this still the reason American lives are
continuously being lost in wars for Empire to control the
social and economic systems of the world?

The Historical and Mythological Basis of Christianity

Thomas Jefferson, the greatest democratic visionary
of all time, also said:

*"I have examined all the known superstitions of
the world, and I do not find in our particular superstition
of Christianity one redeeming feature. They are all
alike founded on fables and mythology. Millions of
innocent men, women and children, since the introduction
of Christianity have been burnt, tortured, fined and
imprisoned. What has been the effect of all this coercion?
To make one-half the world fools and the other half
hypocrites; to support roguery and error all over the earth."*

Some members of the greatest con-artist industry of
all time hold that Jefferson didn't say this, but as I will show
later Christianity, i.e., the greatest con artist industry of all

time, is a lie!

Thomas Paine, 1737-1809, another extremely great democratic visionary and founder of America said:

"The Christian religion is a parody on the worship of the sun, in which they put a man called Christ in the place of the sun, and pay him the adoration originally payed to the sun."

What were Thomas Jefferson and Thomas Paine talking about? Let us examine this question. If one Googles the phrase:" Explaining Why Christianity is False," one can find a 3 part U-Tube [each lasting about 10 minutes] under that phrase and one can learn from this 3 part U-Tube some very revealing facts about the fraudulence of the Christian "lie."

Another very similar [it is virtually the same except it leaves out about the first 5 minutes and the last ½ to 1 minute] 3 part U-Tube presentation can be brought up by Googling: "Truth about Religion."

Also, an even better 4 part U-Tube presentation can be brought up by Googling "Bible=Astrology Part1, part 1 of 4 [4:39min], part 2 of 4 [9:49], part 3 of 4 [9:46], part 4 of 4 [8:23]" and "ZEITGEIST – Proves Christianity Wrong, part 1 of 3[10:03], part 2 of 3[9:48], part 3 of 3 [9:57], plus the Zeitgeist movie—122 minutes."

From these we can learn a lot about how Christianity actually came about and what it is actually based on, which is not the truth and the odds are extremely high that it is based on total falsehood.

If we look at the Egyptian religion of 3000 BC, we find that Christianity is a plagiarism [theft] of it. Jesus Christ, like the Egyptian God Horus, was [is] an elaborate allegorical anthropomorphized [spiritually humanized] sun.

The Christian plagiarizers established Jesus Christ in the image of the Egyptian Sun God [Horus] in that like Horus, Jesus was plagiarized as being born on December 25th of a virgin who had been impregnated by a holy ghost nine months before.

Like Horus, Jesus was plagiarized as being pointed out by a star in the east adorned by 3 kings.

This is also in accordance with astrology. The brightest star in the east [Sirus] lines up with the three brightest stars in O'Ryan's Belt [now known and known to the ancients as the three Kings] to point to the spot on earth that the sun rises on December 25th.

[The virgin birth astrologically refers to the constellation Virgo. This constellation is also the constellation Bethlehem, the house of bread symbolized by a beautiful woman virgin].

Like Horus, Jesus was plagiarized as being a prodigal teacher at 12 years of age [The number 12 is replete throughout the Bible].

Like Horus, Jesus was plagiarized as being baptized and beginning his ministry at 30 years of age. This ties back to astrology also, however I don't understand exactly how except that it is tied to a 30-degree angle the sun makes at some significant point.

Like Horus, Jesus was plagiarized to have had 12 disciples [like the 12 constellations of and around the sun] surrounding him, to have performed miracles, to be known as the Lamb of God, the light of God, King of Kings, Son of God, Light of the World, Alpha and Omega etc.

[It is revealing that due to optical illusion the sun can appear to walk on water. That is where the superstition that "Jesus walked on water" came from.]

Like Horus, Jesus was plagiarized as having been betrayed by a disciple, crucified as a result of the betrayal, dead and buried for 3 days [this death astrologically refers to ancient's concept of the three day death of the sun on December 22,23 and 24 on the "southern cross constellation," hence Horace and Jesus can be said to be "crucified on the cross, dead and buried for three days"] and then resurrected [to the ancients the sun is astrologically resurrected December 25 to foreshadow longer days and spring] to rise up to heaven.

[It is revealing that that is where the superstition "born again" came from, i.e., the sun is born again every day of every year and every year on December 25th]. Therefore, it can astrologically be said that Jesus, like Horus, "died on the cross, was dead for three days and then rose again."

The mythical resurrection on Easter is because this is the astrological equinox when the "good" days start being longer than the "evil" night and the superstitiously "good" light of day overcomes the superstitiously "evil" darkness of night since the longer days overcome the shorter nights on the equinox.

In Christian and Egyptian mythology daylight is

"good" or "righteous" and darkness is "unrighteous" or "evil." This "good" daylight from the sun and "evil" darkness from the lack of the sun is a very important Egyptian and Christian mythological and superstitious concept.

The Bible is actually an Astrotheological Literary Hybrid. The literary similarities between the Egyptian religion and the Christian religion are staggering.

Inscribed on the Temple of Luxor in Egypt are: the enunciation, the immaculate conception, the birth by the virgin Isese and the adoration of Horus, the impregnation by the Holy Ghost, [Neph], on and on.

The plagiarism is continuous. The story of Noah's Arc is plagiarized from multiple antecedent sources in mythological history before the Bible. It is ubiquitous throughout the ancient world, i.e., The Epic of Gilgamesh, 2600 BC, and many more.

The story of Moses [the baby in a basket story] is also plagiarized from stories going back to 2250 BC, i.e., Sargon was placed in a basket, set adrift in a river to avoid infanticide and rescued and raised by royalty.

Moses is just another "lawgiver" in a long line of "lawgivers" in mythological history, i.e., Manou of India, Minos of Crete, Mises of Egypt.

The Ten Commandments [with slightly altered phraseology] are taken outright from the Egyptian "Book of the Dead."

Baptism, Afterlife, Final Judgment, Virgin Birth, Death and Resurrection, Crucifixion, Arc of the Covenant,

Circumcision, Saviors, Holy Communion, Great Flood, Easter, Christmas, Passover and many many more came from the Egyptian religion.

The Christian Religion is basically plagiarized from the Egyptian Religion of some 3000 BC.

Justin Martyr, 100-165 AD said:

"When we say that he, Jesus Christ, our teacher, was produced without sexual union, was crucified and died, and rose again and ascended into heaven we propound nothing different from what you believe regarding the songs of [the God] Jupiter."

He also said:

"He was born of a virgin, accept this in common with what you believe of [the God] Perseus."

It is clear that Justin and other early Christians knew how similar Christianity was to the other Pagan religions.

They wrote all this off to the devil. When anyone gets reasonable [or speaks of evidence], the Christian's blame the devil. He [or the phrase "God put it there to test your faith] is their answer to all reason or evidence.

The Idea of transference can be found in the Bible itself: Joseph, in the Old Testament, was a prototype for Jesus, in the New Testament.

They both had:
1. A miracle birth,
2. Joseph had 12 brothers, Jesus had 12 disciples,

3. Joseph was sold for 20 pieces of silver, Jesus was sold for 30 pieces of silver,
4. Judah suggests the sale of Joseph, Judas suggest the sale of Jesus,
5. They both begin their work at the age of 30 and so on.

You have herd about the some 100 million ignorant and superstitious U.S. citizens who believe in the myth of the "end times":

--When the superstitious believe Jesus will drop down from the sky [in defiance or ignorance of the law of gravity] and carry all the "good-faithful" up to heaven and leave all the scientists, reasonable and rational human beings here on earth to "suffer and burn forever. --

This principally comes from: Matthew, 28:20, where the King James Version of the Bible says "I will be with you even to the end of the world."

The term "world" is a mistranslation among many mistranslations of this version of the Bible.

Actually the correct translation is "I will be with you even to the end of the "aeon" or "age."

This refers to the astrological ages, which are approximately 2147 years long each. All 12 of them combine to be some 25,765 years long.

In the beginning of the Bible, people lived in the age of Taurus the Bull. Moses brought in the "new" age of Ayres the Ram and ordered everyone who still revered the Bull calf to murder themselves in order to cleanse the false reverence.

Jesus Christ's purported birth brought in the age of Pieces, the two fish.

This is what the "fish" reference in the life of Jesus, i.e., the fishermen disciples, the feeding of the hordes with bread and "two fish" etc. is all about.

This [unknown to nearly all Christians themselves] is the real meaning of the "fish" on the back of Christian's cars [We are living in God's Sun's age of Pieces, the two fish].

The end of the Pieces Age will be about 2150 AD. This is what the "end times" is really all about.

There were actually many other sun gods, besides Jesus Christ, plagiarized from the Egyptian sun god Horus.

Mithra, of Persia-1200 BC, born of a virgin, born on Dec. 25th, had 12 disciples, performed miracles, dead for three days, resurrected, Sunday Worship;

Dionysus, of Greece-500 BC, born of a virgin, born on December 25th, performed miracles, was "King of Kings, Alpha and Omega," and was resurrected;

Krishna, of India-900BC, born of a virgin, lead to by a star in the east, performed miracles and was resurrected;

Attis, of Greece- 1200 BC, born of a virgin, born on December 25th, crucified, dead for 3 days and resurrected.

Some other examples are:
1. Alcides of Thebes,
2. Mikado of the Sintoos,

3. Beddru of Japan,
4. Hesus or Eros,
5. Bremrillah, of the Druids,
6. Thor, son of Odin, of the Gauls,
7. Cadmus of Greece,
8. Hil and Feta of the Mandaites,
9. Gentaut and Quexalcote of Mexico,
10. Bali of Afghanistan,
11. Jao of Nepal,
12. Wittoba of the Bilingonese,
13. Thammuz of Syria, and very many more.

There were many historians living contemporarily with the fabricated life of Jesus Christ, but none of them knew of or wrote a word about the existence of [the sun God] Jesus Christ. Some of the contemporary historians who knew nothing of Jesus Christ, his miracles, etc. etc. are:

1. Aulius Persibus [60 AD],
2. Columelia [1st century AD],
3. Dio Chrysosborn [c. 40 c. 112],
4. Justus of Tiborius [c. 80AD],
5. Livryr [59 BC-17 AD],
6. Liucanus [03 AD],
7. Lucius Figrus [1st – 2nd century],
8. Petronius [d. 66 AD],
9. Phaedrus [15 BC – 50 AD],
10. Philo Judacus [20 BC- 50 AD],
11. Phlegon [1st century AD],
12. Plievy the elder [23? -69AD],
13. Plutarch [46 AD-119 AD],
14. Pomponius [40 AD], Rufus Curtius [1st century],
15. Quintillan [35 AD – 100 AD],
16. Quintus Curtius [1st century],
17. Senoca [4 BC – 65 AD],
18. Statius Caclicius [1st century AD],

19. Valerius Flaccus [1st century AD],
20. Valerius Maximus [20 AD], and others.

The Christian Apologists try to argue that there were four people: 1. Penne the Younger, 2. Satonius, 3. Tasitus and 4. Josephus who prove the existence of Jesus Christ, which was, in fact, a myth.

The first only referred to a Christ, which, in fact, means an anointed one of which there were dozens purported at the time.

The second and third refer to a Chrestus which also means an anointed one of which there were dozens purported at the time.

The fourth, Josephus, has been proven a forgery for hundreds of years.

The myth of Jesus is proved by other myths.

This however doesn't stop Christians [members of the most spectacular con-artist industry of all time] from asserting it as truth over, over, over and over ad nausea.

There are other fraudulent proofs, I am sure. The Christians lie about that as they lie about everything else.

--Christianity is just not based on truth. Christianity is nothing but a Roman story developed politically.

Jesus was in fact the solar deity of the Gnostic Christian sect and like all other pagan Gods, he was a mythical figure.

It was the political establishment that sought to historize Jesus for social control [social slavery].

By 325 AD in Rome, Emperor Constantine convened the Council of Nicaea. It was during this meeting that the politically motivated Christian doctrines were established, and thus began a long history of Christian bloodshed and spiritual fraud.

And, for the next 16 hundred years the Vatican maintained a political stranglehold over all of Europe.

This lead to such terrible periods as the Dark Ages, the Crusades and the inquisitions.

Christianity, along with all the other theistic belief systems is the fraud of the age. It serves to detach the species from the natural world and likewise each other.

Christianity supports blind submission to authority.

It reduces human responsibility to the effect that God controls everything. And, therefore, terrible crimes can be justified in the name of divine pursuit.

And most importantly it empowers those who know the truth, but use the myth to manipulate and control societies.

Religious myth is the most powerful device ever created, and it serves as the psychological soil upon which other myths can flourish.

A myth is a story that, although widely believed, is false. A myth serves as an orienting and mobilizing story for a people.

The focus is not on its relationship to reality, but on its function. A story cannot function unless it is believed to be true in the community or the nation.

It has not been a matter of debate. If some people have had the "bad taste" to raise the question of the truth of the myth, the keepers of the faith do not enter into debate with them.

They ignore them or denounce them as blasphemers.—["Explaining why Christianity is false"—intellectual slavery--added]

The Truth That Can Be Concluded From the Mythological, Astrological and Historical Basis of the Bible and Christianity

Evidently from the above evidence in 325 AD in Rome, Emperor Constantine [a tyrant] convened the Council of Nicaea to steal the Egyptian Astrologically based Sun worship mythology and the Gnostic worship mythology and to alter them in the fashion now known as Christianity by changing key names and phraseology to come up with the Bible and all the Christian myths.

Then they taught it to the Roman children as the truth. They also came up with a fabrication of a proof and taught it to the Roman children as the truth. With this thusly produced Christian mythology, the Roman tyranny came up with the greatest tool for tyranny of all time while at the same time it came up with the most spectacular Con Artist industry of all time.

It also is evident from the above evidence that if one goes back to the actual time, i.e., 1 A.D., that Jesus was supposed to have existed, no historian of that time period recorded anything about the existence of Jesus.

At one time the United States was based on the greatest democratic vision of all time: that vision of the greatest democratic visionary of all time was basically the vision of Thomas Jefferson.

Due to the hard fanatic work of the super sales personnel selling sun worship mythology [the most spectacular con artist industry of all time] some 86% [according to a survey of 1990] and some 76% [according to a survey of 2008] of the citizens of the United states have paid trillions of dollars tax free to buy into this terrible mythology.

This turned America from a country based the Jeffersonian democratic vision to a country based on sun worship mythology, which was historized and put in place by Roman tyrants for the function of tyranny.

America is going downhill fast, and the con artists industry must be stopped.

Today, December 2008, Christians [the most spectacular con artist industry of all time] are proselytizing that the United States has a national religion, i.e., secular humanism, there is no wall of separation between church and state, and the national religion should be Christianity [the most spectacular con artist industry of all time]. [This is not withstanding the fact that less than 14% -24% of U.S. citizens claim to be secular humanists and the dictionary definition of *secular* is: **1a**: of or related to the worldly or temporal<~concern> **b**: not overtly or specific. religious <~music> **c**: not ecclesiastical or clerical <~courts><~landowners> **2**: not bound by monastic vows or rules…].

It is time to start telling the truth.

1.   Truth: ***there is*** ***no ancient perfect all-knowing guru from who flows all the perfect unchangeable truth.***

2.   Truth: the only way to the truth is science and the scientific methods.

3.   Truth: Christianity and other theistic religions are vicious, complex and terrible *lies put in place for the function of enslavement*. They are not innocent "goody goody white lies." Christianity is a *terrible lie* plagiarized and historized by Roman tyrants with the intended function of a few men having enslavement over humankind.

4.   Truth: there is no devil "supernatural" or otherwise to blame for all evidence, truth or anything else.

5.   Truth: there is no heaven, "supernatural" or otherwise. This is a myth and nobody will go [or has gone] to heaven. [Of course someone could name a place on earth heaven, but that would not be the heaven of the Bible]

6.   Truth: there is no hell, "supernatural" or otherwise. This is a myth and nobody will go [or has gone] to hell. [The hell of the Bible]

7.   Truth: we are all part of the natural world, i.e., DNA proves that all humans are apes.

[Scientists have repeatably shown some 90 thousand consecutive times that human DNA is 99.4% identical to chimpanzee DNA].

8. Truth: the natural world is the only world there is.

9. Truth: there is no actual detachment from the natural world or other humans; that has never been real but only imaginary and it is a grave mistake for anyone to imagine there is such a detachment.

10. Truth, humans are fully responsible for their actions. If humans do terrible crimes in the *false* name of "divine pursuit," they are terrible criminals.

11. Truth: there is no God that is responsible for anything; humans are responsible for everything they do.

12. Truth: the natural world brings about disasters such as tornados, earth quakes etc.; no God has anything to do with it.

13. Truth: it is totally a hypocritical falsehood for a United States citizen to claim that he [or she] is both a Christian and a free person.

14. Truth: A person can only be free if that person is not a Christian or a believer in a theistic worship system or another sun worship system.

15. Truth: It was a big mistake for the United States to think it could allow religion to exist and to keep America free by forming a "Wall of separation between church and state." Tyrants know that all they have to do is tear down that wall and they can

obtain tyranny over the citizens of the U.S.A.

16. Truth: Tyrants also know they can tear down that wall by convincing people that the U.S.A. is already a religious state and the religion is secular humanism while it should be Christianity [Christians proselytize this with a strait face even though it is well known that less than 14%-24% of the U.S. population claim to be secular humanists...], [Christianity is well known to be the claimed religion of some 76% - 86% of the U.S. citizens and the dictionary definition of *secular* is: **1a**: of or related to the worldly or temporal<~concern> **b**: not overtly or specific. religious <~music> **c**: not ecclesiastical or clerical <~courts><~landowners> **2:** not bound by monastic vows or rules...]. They also know they can trash the Constitution, and they are doing just that.

17. Truth: we must start spreading the actual truth that Christianity and all theistic religions are lies plagiarized by tyrants to enslave citizens.

For most people, such as myself, living in the environment of the zealous super salesmanship of the Christian con artist industry and being proselytized so zealously, it is hard to figure out that Christianity is a total lie.

By the time a person finally figures it out, that person has usually spent a lifetime with a highly loved spouse, children and later on grandchildren celebrating joyous

Christian events such as Christmas [the winter solstice], Advent [the four weeks before the winter solstice], Easter [the spring equinox] etc.

And the spouse and most of the children are totally taken in by the con artist industry and have no desire to get out or listen to any other way of thinking, and the person is lucky if the marriage remains in effect and the spouse and children still love the person.

Before the U.S., a person that figured out the truth was likely put to death. The United States desperately needs to stop teaching total falsehood and start teaching only what is true or the most valid of scientifically irrefutable fact such evolution, the known irrefutable laws of physics, chemistry, biology, other sciences, actual and factual history, English, other languages, our actual laws, how to read, write, math, etc..

There is no justification for the U.S. to continue allowing the Christian con artist industry to continue to perpetrate its fraud [tax free] enabling tyranny in America.

We are supposed to be a free country that allows no form of tyranny or dictatorship, which the Christian con artist industry is.

For a long time I didn't know who the tyrants are that are behind this unbelievable effort to tyrannize the U.S.A., but I could see that they, whoever they were, were successfully tyrannizing us by the very fact that some 76% - 86% of Americans claim to be taken in by this most spectacular con artist industry [for tyranny] of all time.

Now I strongly believe it is our privately owned

central bank(s), i.e., the Federal Reserve System and
the corporations that have been brought forth by them
[as Jefferson warned us about], and I believe they and
the international central bankers of the world have been
enslaving us since 1913.

According to the Wikipedia of March 30, 2009,
virtually every country and certainly the U.S.A., Canada,
Australia, New Zealand, Austria, Belgium, Cyprus, Finland,
France, Germany, Greece, Ireland, Italy, Luxembourg, Malta,
Netherlands, Portugal, Slovakia, Slovenia, Spain, Bulgaria,
Czech Republic, Denmark, Estonia, Hungary, Latvia,
Lithuania, Poland, Romania, Sweden, United Kingdom,
China, Japan, India, and virtually every other country have
privately owned central banks and have virtually known
nothing else.

Before 1913 the United States of America did not
have a Central Bank, and we had an honest monetary system
[From 1750-1913--for 163 years a dollar remained a dollar,
but since 1913 the value of the dollar has declined some
96%--a quarter is now worth some 1 cent in terms of the
money value of 1750-1913]. Also, before 1913 the United
States had virtually no national debt, but after 1913 the U.S.
debt started going up astronomically.

Actually, I distinctly remember when I was around
nine years of age, i.e., 1940, I could, where I lived, buy
a hamburger worth some $5.00 today including a bun,
hamburger meat patty, lettuce, tomatoes, onions, pickles and
mustard for ten cents and a hot dog worth some $5.00 today
including a bun, wiener [later cut in half], chili, onions and
mustard for five cents. So, in some areas I conclude a dollar
went much further than 25 to one, i.e., 50 to one or more.

This plus the Jeffersonian and Adam Smith [read Milton Freedman's *"Freedom of Choice*] approach to the economy and a wonderfully operating U.S. Patent System, which actually promoted progress in science and the useful arts as the Constitution requires enabled us to be the greatest producer and manufacturer in the world.

As evidence of this: In 1939 virtually everything I knew of was made in the U.S.A.; virtually all the cars on the roads were made in the U.S.A.; nearly all the oil was produced in the U.S.A.; it was said we had 75% of the worlds wealth etc.

Today, Panama is about the only country with no central bank, but they don't have our Constitution being carried out.

The lack of questioning the con-artist industries [that get away with it], has to stop, and we the truly free people of America must stand up to these fraud purveyors, i.e., to this con-artist industry and argue truths to them in their face.

In other words, a few hundred years after the anthropomorphized sun, "Jesus Christ" was fraudulently supposed to have walked the earth, the Roman Emperor and leadership decided to plagiarize the Gnostic Pagan Christian Sect [con artist industry] and combine it with the Egyptian Religion [Con-Artist Industry], replacing the name Horus with the name Jesus Christ [and changing other names and appropriately altering the Egyptian writings while keeping their principles to come up with the Bible] and to historize the myth in order to intellectually enslave [create a tyranny over] its citizens for easy and complete control of them.

The Christian leaders of the United States are

following suit. They are simultaneously destroying the wall of separation between church and state. After doing this they intend to use the most spectacular Con Artist Industry of all time to virtually destroy the United States as a free nation in order to gain tyranny for themselves or someone, i.e., the central bankers of the U.S. and/or the world.

Today, February, 2009, there is a Jewish man [named Bernard Madow] living in great disgrace as a Con Artist who used a "Ponzi scheme," [like our Social Security System; i.e., see Walter Williams' article in his syndicated column, of February 4, 2009, set up by one of our con artist presidents], to con investors out of some 52 billion dollars.

The Christian Con Artists have conned people out of multi-trillions of dollars, the governments into making these multi-trillions tax-free [none of this, i.e., income tax or tax-free con artistry, was spelled out or anticipated by the constitution or anticipated by the founding fathers.

Actually, it is contrary to the first amendment of the Bill of Rights, Article VI and other parts of the Constitution] , and over 16 centuries these con artists have caused multi-millions of murders, individuals to be tortured, great loss of freedom, and liberty [inalienable rights], which, in fact, have been perfect crimes [they got away with it], so far.

Christianity is an elaborate myth perpetrated by con artists with the intended function of social slavery [tyranny], yet some 258 million U.S. citizens claim to live under the myth or delusion of Christianity while also claiming *the lie* that they are a free people. These some 258 million people have been taken in [hook, line, and sinker] by the most spectacular con-artist industry of all time.

People will often argue: Well, even if Christianity is a lie, it is the basis of all "good" people's moral behavior.

The Bible is not a good moral guide: Take the Fourth Commandment as an

Example 1:
"Remember the Sabbath day, and keep it holy. For six days you shall labour and do all your work. But the seventh day is to the Lord your God; you shall not do any work –you, your son or daughter, your male or female slave, your live stock or the alien residents in your towns.'— Exodus 20:8-9

GOD COMMANDS NO ONE WORKS ON THE SABBATH DAY!

But, look what goes on in the United States; the following [some of which are now (in 2009) bankrupt because of the Fed.] require their employees or representatives to work on the Sabbath,
1. Wal-Mart
2. Target
3. Best Buy
4. Circuit City
5. The Home Depot
6. Lowe's
7. Burger King
8. Block Buster
9. Jiffy Lube
10. Dick's Sporting Goods
11. McDonalds
12. Office Max
13. Petsmart
14. Taco Bell

15. Toys R Us
16. Denny's
17. IHOP's
18. Even Family Christian Stores
19. Virtually all oilfield workers have to work on the Sabbath. Oil Well drilling rigs must operate 24-7 or the drill pipe will be frozen in the hole. All Service Companies serving drilling rigs must work on the Sabbath on and on.
20. Farmers are forced to work on the Sabbath to avoid loosing their crops and livelihood.
21. I happen to be an inventor [holder of dozens of patents], an artist [drawer and painter], and a writer; so, I know something about creative people with creative ideas. If you are creative you have to act when you get a creative idea; so, you must work on the Sabbath; so, inventors, artists and writers work on the Sabbath also;

On, on & on!

All the above are just some who work on the Sabbath! God commands that we don't work, but we work! What should we do with people who work on the Sabbath day? God, i.e., the writer(s) of the Bible, doesn't even know about guns [Christians can't have it both ways. They can't hold that God wrote the total truth that is all in the perfect Bible, while, at the same time, holding that God, who is all knowing and perfect knows imperfect modern things that aren't in the Bible]; so, we can't shoot them!

What should we do with the people who work on the Sabbath? They are clearly breaking the Ten Commandments that Scalia and his kind all claim is the very basis of America! The Bible demands that we "stone them to death!" Yes, "stone them to death!"

"For six days work is to be done but the Sabbath day is Sabbath of rest, holy to the LORD, whosoever does any work on the Sabbath day <u>must be put to death."</u>—Exodus 31:15—<u>That's right: must be put to death!</u>

The Bible <u>demands the death penalty</u> for multi hundreds of millions [probably 80%, i.e., 240 million] of Americans. How do we kill them? The Bible knows nothing of guns or bullets; so, we can't shoot them. How do we kill them? The Bible knows nothing of gas chambers; so, we can't gas them to death. So how do we kill them?

Can't intelligent, normal people agree that the thought of killing over 100s of millions of Americans over something as trivial as working on the Sabbath is **REPULSIVE**? The Bible, i.e.. the Christian God is **REPULSIVE! REPULSIVE!**

Make no mistake about it. The Bible, i.e., the Christian God, really means what it says. The Christian God, i.e., the Bible, really means to murder all Wall Mart employees etc. on and on [over hundreds of millions].

Look at this:
"The grass withers; the flower fades; but the word of our God will stand <u>forever</u>."—Isaiah 40:8. It also says: "The law of the LORD is <u>perfect</u> "—Peter 1:24-25. Since the laws of the Bible are <u>perfect</u> they should never change.

It should be pointed out that Christians are always using the "*<u>perfect stand forever"</u>* Bible to prove that the scientifically irrefutable theory of evolution is false.

But they fail to acknowledge that they just as validly could use the "*<u>perfect stand forever</u>*" Bible to prove that the existence of guns, bullets, planes, trains, ships, rockets, germs or any of the some 6 million inventions on record in the U.S. Patent Office is false also. The "*perfect stand forever*" Bible knows nothing of any of these things.

Do you believe that over hundreds of millions of Americans should be murdered for working on the Sabbath? If you think this is **REPULSIVE,** you are an intelligent, normal human being. The Bible, i.e., the Christian God, is **REPULSIVE.** Do you want a **REPULSIVE** book, i.e., a God, like this to be **UNCONSTITUTIONALLY** used in our courts of law, in our swearing in ceremonies in breach of the Constitution?

Example 2

The Bible, i.e., the Christian God, wants us to kill even more Americans. Look at the First Commandment:
"Thou shalt have no other gods before me."
What are we supposed to do with everyone who believes the truth and doesn't believe in God or who believe in another God? We are supposed to kill them! Yes!!

"Take the man or woman who has done this evil deed to your city gate and stone that person to death."— Deuteronomy 17:2-7

Deuteronomy 13:13-19, says: If a town doesn't believe in God "…you must attack that town and completely destroy all its inhabitants, as well as all the livestock. Then, you must pile the plunder in the middle of the street and burn it."

Leviticus 24:16 says, "Anyone who blasphemes the name of the LORD must be put to death. The entire assembly must stone him."

The Bible is extremely clear on this. WE MUST KILL EVERYONE WHO DOES NOT BELIEVE IN GOD!

If we actually listen closely to what priests and preachers actually say, it is clear that even they, don't, in truth, actually believe there is a God.

1. If they truly believed there is a God, they would want everyone taught the full truth about everything.
2. They wouldn't want the truth ever withheld from the people at all.
3. They would be totally behind true science [not myth they say is science] because they would know that ultimately true science would irrefutably prove there is a God.
4. But actually they want to withhold the truth, especially the scientifically irrefutable truths such as evolution, because:
5. They, in fact, know there is no God and their ticket to fleecing money, power, prestige, control and influence is threatened by the truth, especially the scientifically irrefutable truth.
6. On the contrary, scientists truly seek the truth and people seeking the truth do not threaten them, unlike priest and preachers.
7. If the Pope truly believed there is a God, he would not be driving around in a *non-biblical* bulletproof automobile.
   a. He drives around in the bulletproof automobile because he knows he is an ape just like all other humans.

b. Further, he knows that if he gets hit by a *"non perfect" non-biblical* bullet, he will die just like any other ape.

If you are a thoughtful, intelligent person, this tells you something. The Bible, i.e., God, is **REPULSIVE!**

Psalm 19:7: "The Law of the LORD is perfect. If you are an intelligent, normal person, you are beginning to see something. The LORD is not perfect, he is **REPULSIVE!**

Example 3

"All who curse their father or mother must be put to death."—Leviticus 20:9

This is **REPULSIVE!**

Example 4

"If a man commits adultery with another man's wife—with the wife of his neighbor—both the adulterer and adulteress must be put to death"—Leviticus 20-10

This is **REPULSIVE!**

Example 5

"If a man lies with a man as one lies with a woman, both of them have done what is detestable. They must be put to death."—Leviticus 20:13

THE BIBLE, I.E., THE CHRISTIAN GOD, DEMANDS THAT WE KILL OVER HUNDREDS OF MILLIONS OF INNOCENT AMERICANS. THE BIBLE, I.E., THE

CHRISTIAN GOD IS REPULSIVE!
THIS IS REPUSLSIVE!

The idea that people are walking around carrying a book that demands the death of over hundreds of millions of innocent people is **REPULSIVE!**

Example 6

Rebellious teenagers must be put to death also:

"If someone has a stubborn and rebellious son who will not obey his father and mother, who does not heed them when they discipline him, then his father and his mother shall...say to the elders of his town, 'This son of ours is stubborn and rebellious. He will not obey us. He is a glutton and drunkard.' Then all the men of the town shall stone him to death."—Deuteronomy 21

Example 7

Comes strait from Jesus—Matthew 18:7-9, Jesus said: "If your hand or your foot cause you to sin, cut it off and throw it away. It is better for you to enter life maimed or crippled than to have two hands or two feet and be thrown into eternal fire. And if your eye causes you to sin , gouge it out and throw it away. It is better for you to enter life with one eye than to have two eyes and be thrown into the fire of hell."

This passage is **REPULSIVE!** On three levels:
1. It is **REPULSIVE** because Jesus is such an idiot here. He is completely wrong. Cutting off your hand or gouging out your eye accomplishes nothing.
2. It is **REPULSIVE** because it demands that people maim themselves.

3. It is **REPULSIVE** because the entire concept of "hell" is **REPULSIVE**.

THE BIBLE, I.E., THE CHRISTIAN GOD, IS REPULSIVE!

Example 8

The Bible's, i.e., the Christian God's, absolute sexism is well known, and is **REPULSIVE!**

We will look at two examples of this:

"Women should remain silent in the churches. They are not allowed to speak, but must be in submission, as the law says. If they want to inquire about something, they should ask their own husbands at home; for it is disgraceful for a woman to speak in the church."—1 Corinthians 14

"Let a woman learn in silence with all submissiveness. I permit no woman to teach or to have authority over men; she is to keep silent."—Timothy 2

REPULSIVE!

There are dozens of passages such as these. The Bible's sexism is both ridiculous and **REPULSIVE!**

Example 9

The Bible, i.e., the Christian God, fully supports slavery!!

The Bible was actually used in the American Civil War as the authoritative justification of slavery and to justify slavery in many other circumstances.

"Your male and female slaves are to come from the nations around you; from them you may buy slaves. You may also buy some of the temporary residents living among you and members of their clans born in your country, and they will become your property. You can will them to your children as inherited property and can make them slaves for life."—Leviticus 25:44

"If a man beats his male or female slave with a rod and the slave dies as a direct result, he must be punished, but he is not to be punished if the slave gets up after a day or two, since the slave is his property."—Exodus Chapter 21:20

"Bid slaves to be submissive to their masters and to give satisfaction in every respect; they are not to be refractory, nor to pilfer, but to show entire and true fidelity."—Titus 2:9

Buying and selling slaves is fine. Beating slaves is fine. Slaves are to show entire and true fidelity.

THE BIBLE IS EXTREMELY CLEAR ON THIS!

If you are a normal, intelligent person, this is extremely **REPULSIVE**. The Bible is **REPULSIVE!**

Example 10

The Bible is riddled with **REPULSION!**

Look at:
"Anyone who is captured will be run through with a sword. Their little children will be dashed to death right before their eyes."—Isaiah 13

Or this:

"Samaria shall bear her guilt, because she has rebelled against her God; they shall fall [by] the sword, their little ones shall be dashed in pieces, and their pregnant women ripped open."—Hasea 13

Or this:

"Now therefore kill every male among the little ones, and kill every woman who has known man by lying with him. But all the young girls who have not known man by lying with him, keep alive for yourselves."—Numbers 31

THE BIBLE IS REPULSIVE!! IT IS NOT THE BASIS OF AMERICA & THE FOUNDING FATHER'S NEVER INTENDED IT TO BE!!

You can find hundreds of repulsive passages in the Bible!

Christian's have mesmerized us into **UNCONSTITUTIONALLY** using the Bible throughout American Society because most Americans have never read the Bible or the Constitution. And have no idea how disgusting the Bible is.

We read from this awful book at Weddings and Funerals. We **UNCONSTITUTIONALLY** force people to put their hands on this book in court. We find copies of the Bible in nearly every hotel and motel room in America.

But by now we should be knowing the truth!

The Bible **DEMANDS** that we:

--Kill everyone who works on the Sabbath.
--Kill teenagers who drink too much
--Enslave people of other nations
--Oppress women
--Kill people who happen to be homosexual
--The list goes on and on.

Additionally: Deuteronomy 22:22-29, states that if a woman is raped she and her rapist must be stoned to death unless she marries her rapist.

Additionally: the Bible, i.e., the Christian God, hates creative people. It states that "Wizards" must be stoned to death. Note: *Leviticus 20:27; it states "A man or woman... that is a wizard shall surely be put to death: they shall stone them with stones: their blood shall be upon them."*

Thomas Edison [who was also smart enough to be an outspoken atheist] was known as "*the Wizard of Menlo Park.*" So, if Edison had been unfortunate enough to live in a Christian nation, he would have been stoned to death. And, America would have been multi billions of dollars poorer in multiple ways.

Creative people built America before Wilson, Roosevelt and the Central Bankers began the destruction of America. The Bible loves sheep; psalm 23. Sheep are easily fleeced and slaughtered. This is the kind of creatures the Bible, i.e., the Christian God, loves.

Additionally there are passages such as Isaiah 45:7; " I form the light, and create darkness: I make peace and create evil; I the Lord do all these things."

And;

Exodus 34:14; "For thou shalt worship no other god; for the Lord, whose name is ***Jealous***, is a ***jealous*** God."

And,
Leviticus 11:22-11; "Even these if them ye may eat; the locust after his kind, and the bald locust after his kind, and the beetle after his kind, and the grass hopper after his kind."

A book this **REPULSIVE** has no place in our society. It is time for the intelligent, thoughtful people of this nation to acknowledge this simple fact and act on it.

I must admit that I have been in a Bible Study group for only a short period of time studying Genesis and could not stand [the absurdity] of even that; so, I dropped out.

But, I wonder: What goes on in Bible Study Groups all over America? What are they doing? If they were honestly studying the Bible, they would be learning just how **REPULSIVE** the Bible really is.

In Bible Study groups they seem to become brain dead and/or often leave out all the distasteful [but more prominently Biblical] parts of the Bible, while saying and implying that everyone must follow the Bible to the letter.

Actually [as more fully discussed above] over hundreds of millions of people work on the Sabbath in the United States, i.e., Wal-Mart employees, Target employees, Best Buy employees, McDonald employees, Burger King employees, oil field workers, farmers etc. on and on.

According to the Bible [and its Ten Commandments] these people must be murdered by stoning [actually from the Bible, i.e., the Christian God, as the ***perfect all knowing guru***, one could prove such things mentioned above, i.e., that modern techniques of murdering people such as shooting them with bullets from guns don't even exist, because the Roman rulers of 325 AD actually plagiarized the Bible from a Gnostic pagan Christian sect and the Egyptian sun god worship system of 3000 BC which knew nothing of these, then unknown, modern inventions].

Also, according to the Bible nobody has inalienable rights and the exercise of these rights would require stoning the exerciser to death.

The Bible is full of such passages as a woman who has been raped [along with her rapist] must die by stoning, children who talk back to their parents must die by stoning etc., but American "Christians" ignore these things and come up with all kinds of fantasies [they can each rationalize by lying to themselves] about what the Bible actually means.

It is mind boggling that a book like the Bible can be cited as the ultimate moral guide. People who do that have to be so brainwashed and indoctrinated that they are virtually brain dead.

Of course, we must hold on to our good cultural habits and customs such as "do unto others as you would have them do unto you," but a much better basic moral guide would be, the Declaration of Independence, Constitution, and Bill of Rights and/or Table 1 below:

Ethical Atheists' Ten Commandments
1. Thou shalt not believe all thou art told.
2. Thou shalt constantly seek knowledge and truth.
3. Thou shalt educate thy fellow man in the Laws of Science.
4. Thou shalt not forget the atrocities committed in the name of God.
5 Thou shalt leave valuable contributions for future generations.
6. Thou shalt live in peace with thy fellow man.
7. Thou shalt live this one life thy have to its fullest.
8. Thou shalt follow a personal code of ethics.
9. Thou shalt maintain a strict separation between Church and State.
10. Thou shalt support those who follow these commandments.

Table 1

The concepts of inalienable rights, liberty and the pursuit of happiness did not come from the Bible. These concepts are completely foreign to the Bible.

They were derived by the principles of Jefferson, the Declaration of Independence, Madison, the Constitution, other founders, and the Bill of Rights.

Christians see gaining total control of the United States as their ticket to converting everyone in the world to the Christian Delusion and murdering everyone they consider not convertible.

This is why they must be defeated and stopped for good. All this, just to enrich and give power, prestige, control and influence to the Christian leadership [really the central bankers of the U.S. and most likely the world], who from what they say with their own words know there is really no God at all.

George Carlin put it starkly well when he said something like the following:

--_I've got to tell you the truth folks. I've got to tell you the truth! When it comes to bullshit, big time, major league bullshit; you have to stand in awe at the all time champion of false promises and exaggerated claims: Religion! Think about it! They have actually convinced people:_
1. _There is an invisible man in the sky._
2. _He watches everything you do every minute of every day!_
3. _He has a list of 10 things he does not want you to do!_
4. _If you do any of these ten things, he has a place he will send you!_
5. _In this place you will burn, suffer, be in pain forever and ever until the end of time!_
6. _But, he loves you!_
7. _He loves you and he needs money!_
8. _He is all-powerful, all knowing, all perfect, and all wise!_
9. _Somehow? He just can't handle money!_
10. _Religion takes in trillions upon trillions of dollars._
11. _They pay no taxes and somehow they always need a little more!_
12. _You talk about a good bullshit story! Holy shit! –_

Let's take a look at the Bible's account of the creation of the world [universe].

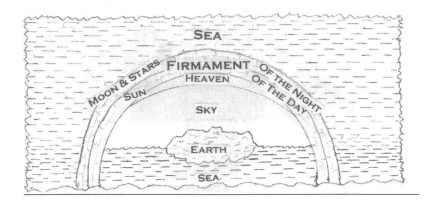

Figure 1.
The "Creationist's, i.e., Intelligent Designer's" Literal Universe: "Genesis: 7; And God made the firmament, and divided the waters which were under the firmament from the waters which were above the firmament: and it was so. "

The Creation

1. *In the beginning God created the heaven and the earth.*
2. *And the earth was without form, and void; and darkness was upon the face of the deep. And the Spirit of God moved upon the face of the waters.*
3. *And God said, Let there be light: and there was light.*
4. *And God saw the light, that **it was** good: and God divided the light from the darkness.*

5. *And God called the light Day, and the darkness he called Night. And the evening and the morning were the first day.*

6. *And God said, let there be a firmament in the midst of the waters, and let it divide the waters from the waters.*

7. *And God made the firmament, and divided the waters which **were** under the firmament from the waters which **were** above the firmament: and it was so.*

8. *And God called the firmament Heaven. And the evening and the morning were the second day.*

9. *And God said, Let the waters under the heaven be gathered together into one place, and let dry **land** appear: and it was so.*

10. *And God called the dry **land** Earth; and the gathering together of the waters called he Seas: and God saw **it was** good.*

11. *And God said, Let the earth bring forth grass, the herb yielding seed, **and** the fruit tree yielding fruit after his kind, whose seed **is** in itself, upon the earth: and it was so.*

12. *And the earth brought forth grass, **and** herb yielding seed after his kind, and the tree yielding fruit, whose seed **was** in itself, after his kind: and God saw and **it was** good.*

13. *And the evening and the morning were the third day.*

14. *And God said, Let there be lights in the firmament of the heaven to divide the day from the night; and let them be for signs, and for seasons, and for days, and years:*

15. *And let them be for lights in the firmament of the heaven to give light upon the earth: and it was so.*

16. *And God made two great lights; the greater light*

to rule the day, and the lesser light to rule the night: he **made** the stars also.

17. *And God set them in the firmament of the heaven to give light upon the earth.*

18. *And to rule over the day and over the night, and to divide the light from the darkness: and God saw that it was Good.*

19. *And the evening and the morning were the forth day.*

20. *And God said, Let the waters bring forth abundantly the creatures that hath life, and fowl that may fly above the earth in the open firmament of heaven.*

21. *And God created great whales, and every living creature that moveth, which the waters brought forth abundantly, after their kind, and every winged fowl after his kind: and God saw that it was good.*

22. *And God blessed them, saying, Be fruitful, and multiply, and fill the waters in the seas, and let fowl multiply in the earth.*

23. *And the evening and the morning were the fifth day.*

24. *And God said, Let the earth bring forth the living creatures after his kind, cattle, and creeping things, and beast of the earth after his kind: and it was so.*

25. *And God said, Let us make man in our image, after our likeness: and let them have dominion over the fish of the sea, and over the fowl of the air, and over the cattle, and over all the earth, and over every creeping thing that creepeth upon the earth.*

26. *So God created man in his own image, in the image of God created he him; male and female*

created he them.

27. *And God blessed them, and God said unto them,*
Be fruitful, and multiply, and replenish the earth,
and subdue it: and have dominion over the fish
of the sea, and over the fowl of the air, and over
every living thing that moveth upon the earth.

28. *And God said, Behold, I have given you every*
herb bearing seed, which is upon the face of all
the earth, and every tree, in the which is the fruit
of a tree yielding seed; to you it shall be for meat.

29. *And to every beast of the earth, and to every fowl*
of the air, and to everything that creepeth upon
the earth, wherein there is life, I have given every
green herb for meat: and it was so.

30. *And God saw every thing that he made, and,*
behold, it was very good. And the evening and the
morning were the sixth day.

Believe it or not I have had Christians say to me: "Your problem is you don't read the Bible. Read it, you will be overwhelmed at how true it is if you just bother to read it."

Lets objectively [without the prejudices of religious leadership] read and more closely examine: "The Genesis Creation:" In Genesis 1. It states: *"In the beginning God created the heaven and the earth."* OK, where does God create the *"heaven and the earth?*

One very weird thing about the Genesis Creation is that the "waters" or "sea" clearly existed before God's creation. In Genesis 2, he said: *"darkness was upon the face of the deep."* Deep what? Later in Genesis 2 it States: *"the Spirit of God moved upon the face of the waters."*

Later in Genesis 6. It states: *"And God said, let there*

be a firmament in the midst of the waters, and let it divide the waters from the waters."

Later in Genesis 10: God called the "waters" the "sea," i.e. Genesis 10: "...*the waters called he Seas...* " The "waters" or "sea" clearly, according to Genesis, existed before God's creation.

Starting with "6." Webster's New Collegiate Dictionary, Copyright 1977 by G. & C. Merriam Co., defines "firmament" as follows: "**1**: the vault or arch of the sky." It defines "vault" as follows: "**1 a:** an arched structure of masonry usu. forming a ceiling or roof b: something (as the sky) resembling a vault c: an arched or dome-shaped anatomical structure 2 **a:** a space covered by an arched structure;" It defines an "arch" as follows: "**1:** a typically curved structural member spanning an opening and serving as a support (as for the wall or other weight above the opening)."

It is clear to a rational person from these dictionary definitions that the people who wrote the bible were so backward and ignorant that they thought the sky was a "structural member" that separated "waters" [sea] from above the "structural member, i.e., the firmament" from the "waters" [sea] below the structural member, i.e., the firmament.

According to "8" the "firmament, i.e. arched structural member separating the water above from the water below, is *"heaven"* itself. So God created *"heaven"* in the *"firmament"* underneath the *"Sea."*

According to "9 and 10" the earth is dry land appearing in the sea that is underneath the heaven, i.e., firmament, and separating the sea and earth from the water above the firmament.

According to "1 and 2" God contradictorily created "heaven and earth" before he created light in "3." According to "4 and 5" light and dark is somehow partitioned and God switches the partitioned day and night back and forth each day.

According to "6" the firmament, i.e., heaven, is formed "in the *midst* of the waters," that "divide the water from the waters."

According to "13-18" there are the greater and lesser *lights* *with*in the arched structure, i.e., heaven separating the sea above the firmament from the sea with the earth in it below the firmament. In this "firmament," the "greater" light, i.e., sun, rules the day and the "lesser" light, i.e., moon and stars, rules the night.

As best I can literally interpret the Genesis "Creation," by using dictionary definitions of terms, it seems clear these Genesis verses are telling us that "God" created the universe underneath the sea in a virtual bubble that is protected by a super strong structural "firmament," which contains heaven, the great light, i.e., sun, of the daytime and the smaller lights, i.e., moon and stars, of the nighttime as shown in Figure 1.

Well folks, I read this passage and other Bible passages and they are just not literally true.

Hardly any Christian, who is highly influenced by the prejudices of the Christian leadership, would admit that this is what Genesis clearly states. They believe without true examination that Genesis means: God created the universe from empty space.

It is hard to believe but there are religious fanatics who are at the very heart of the politics that is on the verge of dominating the United States today, who's actions indicate that they:

> *1.*   *Literally* substitute their mythical interpretations of the Genesis passages 11-12 and 20-31 for the scientific facts of ***evolution and natural selection.***
>
> 2.   And the Genesis passages 1-10, 13-19 and 31 for the scientific facts of astrophysics, physics, the earth sciences and other sciences of our education system.

The United States education system has been so utterly destroyed and ruined by the Christian marketers of fraud that according to the above-cited Gallop poll taken May 10-13, 2007, 43% of Americans accept these type of insane creationism passages on their face as the absolute truth.

Some one-third of the some 6,000,000,000 humans on earth have been conned into believing or having faith that the Christian myth is the truth.

What a curse upon the some 1.1 billion rational, intellectually honest, freethinking, reasonable human beings, such as honest scientists and so-called atheists or infidels, free thinkers, naturalists, and secularists, on this earth.

A lie cannot be made into the truth by brilliant marketing, but Christians can and have deceived millions of Americans into believing the Christian myth by brilliant marketing. A myth is a lie that is widely believed and that is what Christianity is.

What is a marketer? The Webster's New Collegiate Dictionary, Copyright 1977 by G. & C. Merriam Co., defines it as " n: one that deals in a market; *esp* : one that markets a specific commodity <the company is a big gasoline ~>." What is a commodity? The Webster's New Collegiate Dictionary, Copyright 1977 by G. & C. Merriam Co., defines it as "**1 a:** CONVENIENCE, ADVANTAGE **b :** something useful or valuable."

The dictionary doesn't say so but people will buy something if they merely believe it is useful or valuable.

The "commodity" or product Christians, Muslims and Jews market is a totally fraudulent belief system.

In this book, I will limit my discussion to primarily the Christian fraudulent belief system since it is the one I know the most about.

There are many variations of how to present the Christian fraudulent belief system ranging from a very mild soft-core presentation that at least tries to accommodate irrefutable scientific truths to an extremely harsh hard-core presentation that totally rejects irrefutable scientific truths.

The presentation made by most Rectors of the Episcopal Church is usually a very mild soft-core presentation that tries to accommodate irrefutable scientific truths. This is by far the most palatable way of presenting it to what I would consider a rational, intelligent and intellectually honest person.

Certain Christian educational academies and evangelical and fundamentalist churches have a very harsh hard-core presentation that totally rejects irrefutable scientific fact. This creates extreme anger in what I would consider a rational, intelligent and intellectually honest person clear down to their toes.

There are a very few ways [probably only one] to generate accurate knowledge. The most important of these are the scientific method of defining natural phenomena and technology such as engineering and various forms of inventing which utilizes natural phenomena to benefit humankind.

Other valid forms of knowledge include teaching valid knowledge, teaching techniques for teaching valid knowledge and knowledge of human rules or laws of how humans can live and work together harmoniously for not only their survival, but also for a fulfilling, satisfying and happy life (actually the scientific method is certainly the best way of coming up with even these kinds of knowledge).

There is a vast difference between science and Christianity (or the Muslim or Jewish religions).

1. Science is totally and completely validated by observed evidence that always is soundly tied back to the five senses, i.e., seeing, hearing, feeling, smelling and tasting.

2. Scientific instruments and mathematics can be and are used, but ultimately everything about science must soundly tie back to the five senses.

3. For example, the human vision can [unaided]

utilize only a very small percentage of the electromagnetic spectrum, but through science and technology and human vision, the entire electronic spectrum can be utilized to make observations to advance scientific knowledge.

4. Until now, science uses no super sales techniques, no mass media marketing techniques, no brainwashing, i.e., indoctrinating, from birth until death to coerce people into believing it, no torture to coerce people into believing it, no murder to coerce people into believing it, no preaching, no threat of eternal torture in hell, and no multibillion dollar bribe of eternal reward in heaven.

5. Christianity is totally and completely based on early century [or Roman Tyrant's] authoritarianism. The basic authority is supposed to be the Bible.

6. This authoritarianism is above shown to be nothing but a myth, i.e., lie. Most often, it, in fact, is fictitiously based on the Bible.

7. Actually Christians cherry pick the passages in the Bible they choose to interpret; interpret them as they please and try to brainwash, market and otherwise persuade as many as possible into believing their particular interpretation.

8. It is just a tool to enable the particular leader to fleece, tax free, people's money, and gain their respect and admiration. Also to gain prestige for themselves and control over their flock.

9. This Bible is so backward it represents such things, as that π is 3 rather than 3.14159265... In fact it is so backward, it doesn't even know about π, but rather states that to determine the circumference one needs to multiply three times the diameter, see I Kings 7:23.

10. Christians will make all kinds of excuses for this fact and will assert, imaginarily, that it really knew but just didn't say so.

11. It also holds that the earth is a four-cornered rectangle with an angel at each corner, i.e., see Revelation 7:1. Again, Christians will assert imaginarily that it really knew but just didn't say so etc.

12. It states in Judges 1:19; "And the Lord was with Judah; and he drave out the inhabitants of the mountain; but could not drive out the inhabitants of the valley, because they had chariots of iron." [this shows how primitive the technology known by the "God" who wrote the Bible really was]

13. In Exodus 35:14; it states: "For thou shalt worship no other god: for the Lord, whose name is Jealous, is a jealous God." [this shows the "God" who wrote the Bible was just like a spoiled child].

14. This Bible "God" knows nothing about modern technology; knows nothing about science, which truly began with Copernicus in the 1500s.

15. *All the axioms of Christianity such as God, the devil, heaven or hell cannot be observed even with*

*the aid of all the scientific tools such as forensic
science, telescopes, microscopes, mathematics etc.*

16. *This means these axioms can only come from the
human imagination. They had to be dreamed
up or, in fact, plagiarized from the imaginary
Egyptian Religion of 3000 BC.*

17. In order to convince people of this terrible
and imaginary fraudulence, Christianity uses
every evil "attitude adjusting" tactic known to
humankind such as:

   a) **Fear,** *i.e., eternal life of torture in hell,*

   b) **Greed,** *i.e., eternal life of reward in
   heaven,*

   c) **Torture here on earth,** *i.e., it tortured
   millions upon millions of people during
   the inquisitions including Galileo
   himself,*

   d) **Murder,** *i.e., it murdered millions upon
   mullions during the thirty years war and
   for 300 years thereafter,*

   e) **Super salesmanship,**

   f) **Mass media promotion,**

   g) **Indoctrination,** *i.e., brainwashing, from
   birth until death etc. From childhood
   Christians are taught that good people
   blindly believe the Christian fraudulent*

belief system and anyone who doesn't blindly believe it is totally evil and will be tortured in hell for eternity.

18. Both Christianity and science ask the same questions.

   a) I have heard Christians fraudulently teach that they ask different questions, i.e.,

   b) Science asks how and Christianity asks why.

   c) In fact they both ask how and why the universe really is? And how and why did the universe actually start?

   d) They both ask how and why life on earth really is? And how and why did life on earth really start?

   e) Science and Christianity give astronomically different answers to these questions.

   f) The scientific explanation of how and why the universe really is and how it started is explained by,

     i. first: the scientific *Law of Material Balance*, or more often called the *Law of Conservation of mass or matter* first introduced by the Father of Chemistry, *Antoine Lavoisier* back in 1778. It has been scientifically irrefutable ever since then. This law basically states that matter is indestructible, i.e., eternal, and ***cannot be created*** or destroyed. ***Therefore, no being, such as God, could possibly create the mass or matter of the universe.***

ii. Second: the scientific ***Law of conservation of energy*** first introduced by ***Julius Mayer*** back in 1841. It has been scientifically irrefutable ever since then. This law basically states that energy cannot be created or destroyed. ***Therefore, no being, such as God, could possibly create the energy of the universe.***

iii. These scientific laws are the very ***most valid of fact*** in the world. If they are not absolute fact, nothing is fact.

iv. It is true that Einstein later proved that energy can be converted to matter and vice versa, but this does not invalidate Antoine Lavoisier's or Julius Mayer's Laws.

v. Millions of humans have been executed in our court system on the basis of "facts" that weren't one-thousandth as valid as these facts, e.g.,

vi. A fact in a court of law can be established by one witness corroborated by another witness;

vii. Whereas for a scientific theory or law to be established, its validity must be established by one or more scientists and is invalid if anyone in the entire scientific community can disprove it over a very long time period, i.e., 229 years in the case of the ***Law of Material Balance*** and 150 years in the case of the ***Law or Theory of Natural Selection***.

viii. Since these facts are scientifically irrefutably they are the truest of true possible, and ***the existence of God is not fact at all; it is merely faith or in fact a vicious lie,*** which is totally not provable,

ix. *This proves that no God created the **universe**.* Therefore, why the universe is and why it came about is that it eternally existed. It is absolutely not creatable.

x. All so-called "creations" are, in fact, mere changes of state or more specifically a new way of putting together matter (or mass), energy and natural phenomena that, each independently, have actually existed and will exist for eternity.

xi. The "Big Bang" represents mere

change of state (similar to ice changing state by melting into water). It does not refute these truest of facts.

xii. According to the "Big Bang," which extrapolates from observed data backward some 13.7 billion years in time, all the mass and energy in the universe after the "Big Bang (change of state)" existed in the universe before the "Big Bang" (change of state). It describes no creation (something from nothing) or scientific refutation of these truest of fact, i.e. scientific laws.

xiii. *Why* the universe was created is that it eternally existed. It is scientifically impossible to create anything.

xiv. This is *why and how* the universe is, i.e., it has always existed and always will exist.

g) Charles Darwin, probably the greatest scientist of all time, introduced the scientific Law or Theory of Natural Selection over 150 years ago. This Law has been scientifically irrefutable for over 150 years.

i. Through application of this Law, scientists have determined that without creating matter (which is eternal though interchangeable with energy) or energy (which is eternal though interchangeable with matter), single cell life [which life probably has always existed and joined with matter and energy] spontaneously occurred *as a change of state of mass and energy* some 2.5-3.5 billion years ago.

ii. (This spontaneous life has been verified by present day experiments) and through this Law evolved *as a change of state of mass and energy* into the extremely complex multibillion cell biological manifestation of the human species of today.

iii. ***Therefore, no being such as the imaginary Christian, Muslim or Jewish God had anything to do with it.***

iv. One can understand *natural selection* better by thinking about dog breeders using *human selection* to breed dogs or horse breeders using *human selection* to breed horses.

v. Nature has a selection process also, i.e., *natural selection.* Therefore *this is the scientific explanation of how and why life started, came about and is.*

h) The Christian, Muslim and Jewish explanation of everything is:

Bridger Daquan

i. That an invisible, silent, odorless, tasteless, untouchable, imaginary and fraudulent God, who is supposed to be an extremely more complex being than humans (and therefore should have taken hundreds of times longer to come about by *natural selection* than humans), instantly sprang up???

ii. (*Which is scientifically impossible, i.e., mass or energy cannot be created*).

iii. (Or eternally existed???)

   1. (*Which is ridiculous because his or her existence has absolutely no purpose since it is scientifically impossible for him or her to create the mass and/ or energy making up the universe)* in otherwise empty space (in complete defiance or ignorance of the laws of conservation of mass and energy) to instantly (or in a few days, i.e., six days) create the universe from empty space, (in complete defiance or ignorance of the laws of conservation of mass and energy) and to do everything and control everything

   2. (Which is impossible because *natural phenomena* control everything and cannot be

suspended or controlled by any power otherwise:

a.　No scientific theory or law could be verified nor
b.　Could any technological device, such as, planes, trains or automobiles, be operative).

3.　They fraudulently hold this super intelligent being created all the species of the earth

a.　(In complete defiance or ignorance of the laws of conservation of mass and energy) rather than

b.　*Natural selection (which is certainly in complete compliance with the laws of conservation of mass and energy by not creating but by changing the state of mass and energy to result in life on earth).*

c.　If, by the wildest stretch of the imagination, one dreamed they could do the scientifically impossible and could possibly be correct to say their fraudulent God designed all creatures,

d. Their fraudulent God is an ***extremely stupid*** designer because science has irrefutably shown that between 99% and 99.9% of all the species that have been on earth are now extinct.

e. This Christian fraud is scientifically impossible and nobody, who has not been made totally brain dead or a delusional addict by years of tyrannical indoctrination could or should possibly believe it.

19. Christians have fraudulently attempted to teach (or indoctrinate) me that:

    a) Science and Christianity are both just belief systems and

    b) That science is nothing but a false belief system with not nearly the validity of the Christian belief system.

20. Christians have fraudulently attempted to teach (or indoctrinate) me that:

    a) A scientific theory or law is not a fact and that:

    b) Christianity is the only truth.

    c) In fact a scientific theory or law is the very

most valid of fact.

d) As stated above millions of humans have been condemned to death in our court systems from "facts" that weren't one-thousandth as valid as a scientific theory or law.

21. It should be pointed out that ***Atomic Theory*** has a long history of development. There is an 8 page article in the Wikipedia that as of July 12, 2007 was last modified 13:56, 11 July 2007, under ***Atomic Theory***. For practical purposes;
    a) One can think of all existence being made up of molecules;

    b) Molecules being made up atoms;

    c) Atoms being made up of protons and neutrons in its nucleus with electrons rotating in orbits around its nucleus.

    d) This has been proven to have unanswered flaws in rare situations.

    e) But essentially: protons, neutrons and electrons are not the fundamental units of existence.

    f) These fundamental units of existence are much smaller, much more difficult to define, and one theory is that they are actually units of energy.

Christians and others have said to me that one cannot

prove there is no God.

I say that, in fact the overwhelming evidence proves: there is

      a.   No power in the universe that can suspend or control any of the natural phenomena

      b.   Otherwise there could be no operative technological device such as an automobile, airplane or the like

      c.   Nor could any scientific theory or law be verified and if it could not be verified, it could not even exist.

      d.   If no such power exists that can suspend or control natural phenomena, there is no God that has any power except the power people, themselves, give it in their imagination to play on their own fear and/or greed within their own brains just as Jimmy Stewart gave Harvey the imaginary rabbit in the 1950s movie: "Harvey."

      e.   According to the first four of the Ten Commandments (as set forth in detail in my book Delusion Addiction) and Bible passages such as Exodus 35:14, God is an extremely jealous, mean, bigoted and vindictive being.

f.   If such a God could suspend or control a natural phenomenon, he would suspend or control the natural phenomena that enable my (or any non-believer's) automobile to operate and I (or any non-believer) would not be able to drive anywhere.

g.   He would suspend or nullify the natural phenomena that enable my computer to work and I would not be able to use it.

h.   Christians have fraudulently said ridiculous things to me such as "oh well he is just being nice; he could if he wanted to."

i.   In fact, this cannot happen.

j.   In fact, there is no being that can suspend any natural phenomena.

k.   The natural phenomena are what control the universe and

l.   In fact there is no being that can suspend or override the natural phenomena that control the universe.

Are "the people" taught the truth, in our schools or by our press, about the most spectacular con-artist industry of all time?

No!! They are taught that if they don't swallow the lies perpetrated by the con-artist industry, hook, line and sinker, they will go to hell and be tortured for all eternity.

And if they do swallow lies perpetrated by the con-artist industry, hook, line and sinker, they will go to heaven to live with "God" in pleasure for all eternity.

Again The Most Spectacular Con Artist Industry Of All Time Is Capable of Doing Terrible Harm to Humans

The Wikipedia of October 20, 2006, states:

"The **Thirty Years' War** was fought between 1618 and 1648, principally on the territory of today's Germany, and involved most of the major European continental powers. Although it was from the outset a religious conflict between Protestants and Catholics, the rivalry between the Habsburg dynasty and other powers was also a central motive, as shown by the fact that Catholic France even supported the Protestant side, increasing France-Habsburg rivalry.

The impact of the Thirty Years' War and related episodes of famine and disease was devastating. The war may have lasted 30 years, but conflicts continued for 300 more years."

It goes on for fourteen pages.

This "Habsburg dynasty" is verification that human tyrants are really behind the tyranny of the religious con artist industry. A man who has done extensive reading about the **Thirty Years' War** told me that at the beginning of this war the German population was some 32,000,000 people; whereas, at the end of that war the German population was some 16,000,000 people. No other war in history wiped out half the population of a country.

The dominant Christian population of the U.S. has worked hard to downgrade the devastation of the Thirty Years' War.

But, if you think it minor that two slightly different **types of con artistry** causing two slightly different delusions of holiness can enrage the delusion pushers, addicts and enablers of each of the different groups so much that even in the ball park of half an entire nation is killed, think again.

Yes, **the Christian Con Artistry** has done and can do extreme harm to humans now as in the past, probably more harm than anything else, and will do extreme harm to humans in the future if we let it.

Again The Most Spectacular Con Artist Industry Of All Time Is Capable of Causing Vast Human Cruelty

It is well known that in the days of the Christian inquisitions, people, without warning, were seized and brought before a judge.

They were asked questions such as: Did you create a thunderstorm that destroyed the village harvest? Did you kill the neighbor with your evil eye? Do you doubt that Christ is bodily present in the Eucharist?

There was no exculpatory answer. The person was guilty regardless of the answer.

The person was not told the names of his or her accusers.

But, the accusers couldn't recant their accusations because they would then be punished for false witness and the accused would still be held guilty as charged.

But, the person (victim) is given the choice of naming his or her accomplices. The person must have accomplices.

No confession is acceptable unless other men and women can be implicated in the imagined crime.

An iron boot designed to crush the person's feet was used to refresh the person's memory until the person named several other imagined accomplices.

The jailers were happy to lead their victims to the furthest reaches of human suffering, before burning them at the stake.

The accused were often imprisoned in total darkness for months or years at a time, repeatably beaten and starved, or stretched upon the rack.

Thumbscrews or toe screws were applied, or a pear shaped vise was inserted into the victim's mouth, vagina or anus, and forced open until their misery admitted of no possible increase.

The person may be hoisted to the ceiling on a

"strappado" (with their hands behind their back and attached to a pulley, and weights tied to their feet), dislocating their shoulders.

To this torment "squassation" might be added, which often caused the person's death. The cruelty capability was endless and terrible.

Again, we must fight the Most Spectacular Con Artist Industry of All Time. This industry has ripped us off of multibillions of tax free dollars, multimillions of human lives and multimillions of humans enduring great suffering.

This has to come to an end.

This industry has detached humans from the natural world and each other. It has caused the unjustifiable slaughter of each other and other animals of the natural world.

It has caused millions upon millions of unnecessary deaths of disease from such ridiculous rules as the prohibition of condom use, birth control, and stem cell use. All this must be stopped.

The so-called "right to life" is not about the right to life. It is about the enslavement of women.

I personally believe the founding fathers of the United States knew the lie of Christianity was a tool for tyrants to make America [or other countries] a tyranny, but they thought it not possible or practical to disallow the existence of the lie of Christianity.

However, they thought they could neutralize the lie of

Christianity as a tool for tyrants to make America a tyranny
by creating a "Wall of Scparation between Church and State."
This did work for a long time, but the tyrants are tearing
down that wall now.

The most important thing that we can learn from all
the above is that the overwhelming majority of United States
citizens are very capable of swallowing total lies hook, line
and sinker despite overwhelming evidence proving they
aren't true.

The truth cannot be made false by prayer, or by refusal by billions of people to believe it, or by having faith that it is not true, or by murdering the truth's revealer, or by torturing the truth's revealer, or by naming him or her a blasphemer, or by brilliant salesmanship, or by mass propaganda or marketing, or by indoctrinating children with untruth from birth until death, or by saying only the devil could cause the truth teller to tell the truth. – Bridger Daquan

Eternal Vigilance is the Price of Liberty, not faith or hope

Chapter III

People and Institutions Who Have Tried To Lead Us To The Truth

The Constitutional basis: Article I
Section 8. The Congress shall have power To promote progress of science and useful arts, by securing for limited times to authors and inventors the exclusive right to their respective writings and discoveries;

The basis of the most spectacular truth telling industry of all time is science. What is science? Science is an extensive, many faceted method of seeking the **TRUTH FROM EVIDENCE. SCIENCE SEEKS TRUTH FROM EVIDENCE!** The Wikipedia of January 6, 2009, states the "Scientific method refers to bodies of techniques for investigating phenomena, acquiring new knowledge, or correcting and integrating previous knowledge. To be termed scientific, a method of inquiry must be based on gathering observable, empirical and measurable evidence subject to specific principles of reasoning. A scientific method consists of the collection of data through observations at experimentation, and the formation and testing of hypotheses. Although procedures vary from one field of inquiry to another, identifiable features distinguish scientific inquiry from other methodologies of knowledge. Scientific researchers propose hypotheses as explanations of phenomena, and design experimental studies to test these hypotheses. These steps must be repeatable in order to dependably predict any further results. Theories that encompass wider domains of inquiry may bind many hypotheses together in a coherent structure. This in turn may help form new hypotheses or place groups of hypotheses into context. Among other facets shared by the various fields of inquiry is the conviction that the process be objective to reduce biased interpretation of results. Although basic expectation is to document, archive and share all data and methodology so they are available for careful scrutiny by other scientists, thereby allowing other researchers the opportunity to verify results by attempting to reproduce them. This practice, called *full disclosure,* also allows statistical measures of the reliability of these data to be established."

In my view science defines the unalterable phenomena that rule the real [natural] world and technology utilizes the unalterable phenomena that rule the real [natural] world.

Some of the greatest contributors to the most spectacular truth telling industry of all time are as follows:

Charles Darwin: The greatest scientist of all time. Darwin originally intended to be a member of the clergy of the Anglican Church. But he was a naturalist, which was approved of by the Anglican Church at that time. Finally, he could not ignore the overwhelming evidence. And, because of the overwhelming ***evidence,*** he reluctantly became the man who originated the theory or law of **Natural Selection**, which was the key to the now termed "evolution of life," itself, from the simplest form of life to the extremely complex human being of today. Darwin developed his interest in natural history while studying first medicine at Edinburgh University, then theology at Cambridge. His five-year voyage on the *Beagle* through the Galápagus Islands established him as a geologist whose observations and theories supported Charles Lyell's uniformitarian ideas. Puzzled by the geographical distribution of wildlife and fossils he collected on the voyage, Darwin investigated the transmutation of species and conceived his theory of natural selection in 1838. He was so intimidated by lying Christians that he didn't actually publish his irrefutable new scientific law or theory until 1859.

Antoine Lavoisier: first introduced the **Law of Material Balance** or more often called **the Law** of **Conservation of mass or matter** back in 1778, after the United States Declaration Independence of 1776. He was the father of Chemistry and one of the all-time greatest scientists. He was a French nobleman prominent in the histories of chemistry, finance, biology, and economics. He also co-discovered, recognized and named oxygen (1778), as well as hydrogen, disproved the phlogiston theory, introduced the *metric system,* wrote the first extensive list of elements, and helped to reform chemical nomenclature. Christians unjustly beheaded him in accordance with their unjust Bible.

Julius Mayer: first introduced the **Law of Conservation of Energy** back in 1841. He was one of the all-time greatest scientists. He was a German physician and physicist and one of the founders of thermodynamics. In 1842 he also described the vital chemical process now referred to as oxidation as the primary source of energy for any living creature. His contributions were overlooked and some say Joule was given credit for some of Mayer's contributions.

Archimedes: [287 BC – c. 212 BC] was a Greek mathematician, physicist, engineer, inventor, and astronomer. Although few details of his life are known, he is regarded as one of the scientists in classical antiquity. He came up with *Archimedes' principle,* which is *the law of Buoyancy*, proving that Jesus Christ or nobody else could have ever walked on water. He did a lot of other things. Among his advances in physics are the foundations of hydrostatics, statics and the explanation of the principle of the lever. He is credited with designing innovative machines, including siege engines and the screw pump that bears his name. Modern experiments have tested claims that Archimedes designed machines capable of lifting attacking ships out of the water and setting on fire using an array of mirrors.

Adam Smith: He was actually one of, if not, the greatest scientist in developing the theory and practice of the operational principles of free enterprise and capitalism. He was one of the key figures in the intellectual movement known as the Scottish Enlightenment and the author of *An Inquiry into the Nature and Causes of the Wealth of Nations (1776).* One of the earliest and best attempts to systematically study the historical development of industry and commerce in Europe, as well as a sustained attack on the doctrines of mercantilism. Smith's work provided one of the best-known intellectual rationales for free trade, capitalism, and libertarianism. He was the first person to shine light on the natural phenomenon of human nature that is a free-enterprise system that along with a good patent system activates human nature to produce the greatest amount of intellectual property, prosperity and general wealth yet known to humankind.

Isaac Newton: [4 January 1643 – 31 March 1727] was an English physicist, mathematician, astronomer, natural philosopher, alchemist, and theologian and one of the most influential men in human history. His *Philosophiæ Naturalis Principia Mathematica,* published in 1687, is considered to be the most influential book in the history of science. In this work, Newton described universal gravitation and the three laws of motion, laying the groundwork for classical mechanics, which dominated the scientific view of the physical universe for the next three centuries and is the basis for modern engineering. Newton showed that the motions of objects on Earth and of celestial bodies are governed by the same set of natural laws by demonstrating the consistency between kepler's laws of planetary motion and his theory of gravitation, thus removing the last doubts about heliocentrism and advancing the scientific revolution. In mechanics, Newton enunciated the principles of conservation of momentum and angular momentum. In optics, he built the first "practical" reflecting telescope and developed a theory of colour based on the observation that a prism decomposes white light into a visible spectrum. He also formulated an empirical law of cooling and studied the speed of sound. He lived in an age dominated by the Christian Con Artist Industry and did not challenge it except through the truth of his scientific revelations.

Albert Einstein: [14 March 1879 – 18 April 1955] was a German born theoretical physicist. He was best known for his theory of relativity and specifically mass-energy equivalence, expressed by the equation $E = mc^2$. Einstein received the 1921 Nobel Prize in Physics "for his services to Theoretical Physics, and especially for his discovery of the law of the photoelectric effect."

Einstein's many contributions to physics include his special theory of relativity, which reconciled mechanics with electromagnetism, and his general theory of relativity, which was intended to extend the principle of relativity to non-uniform motion and to provide a new theory for gravitation. His other contributions include advances in the fields of relativistic cosmology, capillary action, critical opalescence, classical problems of statistical mechanics and their application to quantum theory, an explanation of the Brownian movement of molecules, atomic transition probabilities, the quantum theory of a monatomic transition probabilities, the quantum theory of a monatomic gas, thermal properties of light with low radiation density (which laid the foundation for the photon theory), a theory of radiation including stimulated emission, the concept of unified field theory, and the geometrization of physics. Einstein published over 300 scientific works and over 150 non-scientific works.

Nicolaus Copernicus: [February 19, 1473 – May 24, 1543] was the first astronomer to formulate a scientifically based heliocentric cosmology that displaced the Earth from the center of the universe. His epochal book, *De revolutionibus orbium coelestium (On the Revolutions of the Celestial Spheres),* is often regarded as the starting point of modern astronomy and the defining epiphany that began the scientific revolution. Although Greek, Indian and Muslim savants had published heliocentric hypotheses centuries before Copernicus, his publication of a scientific theory of heliocentrism, demonstrates that the motions of the celestial objects can be explained without putting the Earth at rest in the center of the universe, stimulated further scientific investigations and became a landmark in the history of modern science that is known as the Copernicus Revolution.

Galileo Galilei: [15 February 1564 – 8 January 1642] was a Tuscan physicist, mathematician, astronomer, and philosopher who played a major role in the Scientific Revolution. His achievements include improvements to the telescope and consequent astronomical observations, and support for Copernicanism. Galileo has been called the "father of modern observational astronomy," the "father of science," and "the Father of Modern Science." The motion of uniformly accelerated objects, taught in nearly all high school and introductory college physics courses, was studied by Galileo as the subject of kinematics. His contribution to observational astronomy include the telescopic confirmation of the phases of Venus, the discovery of the four largest satellites of Jupiter, named the Galilean moons in his honor, and the observation and analysis of sunspots. Galileo also worked in applied science and technology, improving compass design. Christians subjected Galileo to inquest and slavery over his support and further proof of Copernicanism and basically made him a humiliated prisoner for the last years of his life and refused to forgive him until 1992.

James Clerk Maxwell: [13 June 1831—5 November 1879] was a Scottish theoretical physicist and mathematician. His most significant achievement was the development of the classical electromagnetic theory, synthesizing all previous unrelated observations, experiments and equations of electricity, magnetism and even optics into a consistent theory. His equations—Maxwell's equations—demonstrated that electricity, magnetism and even light are all manifestations of the same phenomenon: the electromagnetic field. From that moment on, all other classic laws or equations of these disciplines became simplified cases of Maxwell's equations. Maxwell's work in electromagnetism has been called the *"second great unification in physics,"* after the first one carried out by Isaac Newton.

Maxwell demonstrated that electric and magnetic fields travel through space in the form of waves, and at the constant speed of light. Finally, in 1864 Maxwell wrote *A Dynamical Theory of the Electromagnetic Field* where he first proposed that light was in fact undulations in the same medium that is the cause of electric and magnetic phenomena. His work in producing a unified model of electromagnetism is considered one of the greatest advances in physics.

Maxwell also developed the Maxwell distribution, a statistical means to describe aspects of kinetic theory of gases. These two discoveries helped usher in the era of modern physics, laying the foundation for future work in such fields as special relativity and quantum mechanics. He is also known for creating the first true colour photograph in 1861.

Maxwell is considered by many physicists to be the nineteenth century scientist with the greatest influence on twentieth century physics. His contributions to the science are considered by many to be the same magnitude as those of Newton and Albert Einstein. In 1931, on the centennial of Maxwell's birthday, Einstein himself described Maxwell's work as the *"most profound and the most fruitful that physics has experienced since the time of Newton."* Maxwell did many other things also.

Frances Bacon: [22 January 1561—9 April 1626], son of Nicholas Bacon by his second wife Anne (Cooke) Bacon, was an English philosopher, statesman, lawyer, jurist and author. He is considered by many to be the first or among the first advocates of defining the scientific method and using as the primary tool for determining the truth. He served both as an Attorney General and Lord Chancellor of England. Although his political career ended in disgrace, he remained extremely influential through his works, especially as philosophical advocate and practitioner of the scientific revolution. Indeed, his dedication may have brought him into a rare historical group of scientists who were killed by their own experiments.

His works established and popularized an inductive methodology for scientific inquiry, often called the *Baconian method* or simply, the scientific method. His demand for planned procedure of investigating all things natural marked a new turn in the rhetorical and theoretical framework for science, much of which still surrounds conceptions of proper methodology today.

Bacon was knighted in 1603, created Baron Verulam in 1618, and Viscount St Alban in 1621;without heirs, both peerages became extinct upon his death. Bacon did many other great things.

Marie Curie: [November 7, 1867—July 4, 1934] was a physicist and chemist of Polish upbringing and, subsequently, French citizenship. She was a pioneer in the field of radioactivity, the first person honored with two Nobel Prizes, and the first female professor at the University of Paris.

She was born ***Maria Sklodowska*** in Warsaw (then Vistula Country, Russian Empire; now Poland) and lived there until she was 24. In 1891 she followed her elder sister Bronislawa to study in Paris, where she obtained her higher degrees and conducted her subsequent scientific work. She founded the Curie Institutes in Paris and Warsaw. Her husband Pierre Curie was a Nobel co-laureate of hers, and her daughter Irène Joliot-Curie and son-in-law Frédéric Joliot-Curie also received Nobel prizes.

Her achievements include the creation of a theory

of *radioactivity* (a term coined by her), techniques for
isolating radioactive isotopes, and the discovery of two new
elements, polonium and radium. It was also under personal
direction that the world's first studies were conducted into
the treatment of neoplasms ["cancers"], using radioactive
isotopes. She was a brilliant atheist genius and did many
more good things.

Michael Faraday: [22 September 1791—25 August
1867] was an English chemist and physicist (or natural
philosopher, in the terminology of the time) who contributed
to fields of electromagnetism and electrochemistry.

Faraday studied the magnetic field around a conductor
carrying a DC electric current, and established the basis for
the electromagnetic field concept in physics. He discovered
electromagnetic induction, diamagnetism, and laws of
electrolysis. He established that magnetism could affect rays
of light and that there was an underlying relationship between
the two phenomena. His inventions of electromagnetic rotary
devices formed the foundation of electric motor technology,
and it was largely due to his efforts that electricity became
viable for use in technology.

As a chemist, Faraday discovered benzene,
investigated the clathrate hydrate of chlorine, invented an
early form of Bunsen burner and the system of oxidation
numbers, and popularized terminology such as anode,
cathode, electrode, and ion.

Although Faraday received little formal education
and knew little of higher mathematics, such as calculus, he
was one of the most influential scientists in history. Some
historians of science refer to him as the best experimentalist
in the history of science. The SI unit of capacitance, the
farad, is named after him, as is the Faraday constant, the
charge on a mole of electrons [about 96,485 coulombs].
Faraday's law of induction states that a magnetic field

changing time creates a proportional electromotive force.

Faraday was the first and foremost *Fullerton Professor of Chemistry* at the Royal Institution of Great Britain, a position to which he was appointed for life. He was apparently not able to break away from his peer pressure to be taken in by the most spectacular con artist industry of all time, the Christian religion, but he did many other good things.

Niels Bohr: [7 October 1885—18 November 1962] was a Danish physicist who made fundamental contributions to understanding atomic structure and quantum mechanics, for which he received the Nobel Prize in Physics in 1922. Bohr mentored and collaborated with many of the top physicists of the century at his institute in Copenhagen. He was also part of the team of physicists working on the Manhattan Project. Bohr married Margrethe Nørlund in 1912, and one of their sons, Aage Niels Bohr, grew up to be an important physicist who, like his father, received the Nobel Prize, in 1975. Bohr has been described as one of the most influential physicist of the 20th century.

Carl Sagan, Ph.D.: [November 9, 1934—December 20, 1996] was an American astronomer, astrochemist, author, and highly successful populizer of astronomy, astrophysics and other natural sciences. He pioneered exobiology and promoted the Search for Extra-Terrestrial Intelligence [SETI].

He is world-famous for writing popular science books and for co-writing and presenting the award-winning 1980 television series *Cosmos: A Personal Voyage,* which has been seen by more than 600 million people in over 60 countries, making the most widely watched PBS program in history. A book to accompany the program was also published. He also wrote a novel *Contact,* the basis for 1997 Robert Zemeckis film of the same name starring Jodie Foster. During his lifetime, Sagan published more than 600 scientific papers and popular articles and was author, co-author, or editor of more than 20 books. In his works, he frequently advocated skeptical inquiry, secular humanism, and the scientific method. ***Notable Awards:*** Oerted Medal [1990], NASA Distinguished Public Service Medal (twice), Pulitzer Prize for General Non-Fiction (1978).

James Watson [born April 6, 1928] is an American molecular biologist, best known as one of the co-discoverers of the structure of DNA. Watson, Frances Crick, and Maurice Wilkins were awarded the 1962 Novel Prize in Physiology or Medicine "for their discoveries concerning the molecular structure of nucleic acids and its significance for information transfer in living material." He studied at the University of Chicago and Indiana University and subsequently worked at the University of Cambridge's Cavendish Laboratory in England where he first met his future collaborator and personal friend Frances Crick.

In 1956 he became a junior member of Harvard University's Biological Laboratories until 1976, but in 1968 served as Director of Cold Spring Harbor Laboratory on Long Island, New York and shifted its research emphasis to the study of cancer. In 1994 he became its president for ten years, and then subsequently served as its Chancellor until 2007, when he was forced into retirement by controversy over several comments about race and intelligence. Between 1988 and 1992 he was associated with the National Institutes of Health, helping to establish the Human Genome Project. He has written many science books, including the seminal textbook *The Molecular Biology of the Gene* (1965) and his best selling book *The Double Helix* (1968) about the DNA discovery.

Frances Crick [8 June 1916—July 2004] was a British molecular biologist, physicist and neuroscientist, and most noted for being one of the co-discoverers of the structure of the DNA molecule in 1953. He, James D. Watson and Maurice Wilkins were jointly awarded the 1962 Nobel Prize for Physiology or Medicine "for their discoveries concerning the molecular structure of nucleic acids and its significance for information transfer in living material."

Crick is widely known for use of the term "central dogma" to summarize an idea that genetic information flow in cells is essentially one-way, from DNA to RNA to protein. Crick was an important theoretical molecular biologist and played a crucial role in research related to revealing the genetic code.

During the remainder of his career, he held the post of J.W. Kieckhefer Distinguished Research Professor at the Salk Institute for Biological Studies in La Jolla, California. His later research centered on theoretical neurobiology and attempts to advance the scientific study of human consciousness. He remained in this post until his death: "he was editing a manuscript on his death bed, a scientist until the bitter end" said Christof Koch.

This is just a small sample of the millions of scientists who have been working to bring forth the actual truth for the benefit of humankind, and who have been fought tooth and tong by the ubiquitous con artist industries, i.e., religions.

"The Bible is not my book nor Christianity my profession. I could never assent to the long, complicated statements of Christian dogma."—Abraham Lincoln—One of America's last truly great and truly honest presidents—

Chapter IV

People And Institutions Who Have Tried To Improve Our Lives By Utilizing Truth

The Constitutional basis: Article I
Section 8. The Congress shall have power To promote progress of science and useful arts, by securing for limited times to authors and inventors the exclusive right to their respective writings and discoveries;

What has "useful arts" come to mean nowadays? I believe "useful arts" has come to mean patentable inventions applying science, engineering and technology, i.e., networks of inventions such as various fields of engineering, other forms of techniques and other science applications.

The Wikipedia [of January 7, 2009] states: "The distinction between science, engineering and technology is not always clear. Science is the reasoned investigation of phenomena, aimed at discovering enduring principles among elements of the phenomenal world by employing formal techniques such as the scientific method. Technologies are not usually exclusively products of science, because they have to satisfy requirements such as utility, usability and safety. Engineering is the goal-oriented process of designing and making tools and systems to exploit natural phenomena for practical human means, often (but not always) using results and techniques from science. The development of technology may draw upon many fields of knowledge, including scientific, engineering, mathematical, linguistic, and historical knowledge, to achieve some practical result."

Some of the greatest contributors to the most spectacular truth utilizing industry of all time are as follows:

Thomas Edison: [February 11, 1847—October 18, 1931]
Received 1040 U.S. Patents. Edison was an American inventor and businessman who developed many devices that greatly influenced life around the world, including the phonograph and the long-lasting practical light bulb. Dubbed "The Wizard of Menlo Park" by a newspaper reporter, he was one of the first inventors to apply the principles of mass production and large teamwork to the process of invention, and therefore is often credited with the creation of the first industrial research laboratory.

Edison is considered one of the most prolific inventors in history, i.e., note he had 1040 U.S. Patents when America actually had a great patent system, as well as many patents in the United Kingdom, France and Germany. He is credited with numerous inventions that contributed to mass communications and, in particular, telecommunications. His advanced work in these fields was an outgrowth of his early career as a telegraph operator. Edison originated the concept and implementation of electric-power generation and distribution to homes, businesses, and factories—a crucial development in the modern industrialized world. His first power plant was in Manhattan Island, New York. He was brilliant atheist genius and did many other great things.

James Watt: [19 January 1736—25 August 1819] was a Scottish inventor and mechanical engineer whose improvement to the steam engine were fundamental to the changes brought by the Industrial Revolution in both the Kingdom of Great Britain and the world.

James Watt was born 19 January 1736 in Greenock, Renfrewshire, a seaport on the Firth of Clyde. His father was a shipwright, ship owner and contractor, while his mother Agnes Muirhead, came from a distinguished family and was well educated.

Watt did not attend school regularly, but instead his mother, like Edison, mostly schooled him at home. He exhibited great manual dexterity and an aptitude for mathematics, although Latin and Greek left him cold, and he absorbed the legends of lore of the Scottish people.

Henry Ford: [July 30, 1863—April 7, 1947] was the American founder of the Ford Motor Company and father of modern assembly lines used in mass production. His introduction of the Model T automobile revolutionized transportation and American industry plus later worldwide industry. He was a prolific inventor and was awarded 161 U.S. Patents. As owner of the Ford Motor Company he became one of the richest and best-known people in the world. He is credited with "Fordism," that is, the mass production of large numbers of inexpensive automobiles using the assembly line, coupled with high wages for his workers. Ford had global vision, with consumerism as the key to peace. Ford did not believe in accountants; he amassed one of the world's largest fortunes without ever having his company audited under his administration. Henry Ford's intense commitment to lowering costs resulted in many technical and business innovations, including a franchise system that put a dealership in every city in North

America, and in major cities on six continents. Ford left most of his vast wealth to the Ford Foundation but arranged for his family to control the company permanently.

Henry Ford was born July 30, 1863, on a farm next to a rural town west of Detroit, Michigan (this area is now part of Dearborn, Michigan). His father, William Ford (1826—1905), was born in County Cork, Ireland. His mother Mary Litogot Ford (1839—1876), was born in Michigan; she was the youngest child of Belgian immigrants; her parents died when Mary was a child and neighbors, the O'Herns, adopted her. Henry Ford's siblings include Margaret Ford (1867—1938): Jane Ford (c. 1868—1945); William Ford (1871—1917), and Robert Ford (1873—1934).

His father gave Henry a pocket watch in his early teens. At fifteen, Ford dismantled and reassembled the timepieces of friends and neighbors dozens of times, gaining the reputation of a watch repairman.

In 1789, Ford left home to begin his lifelong career. He started out as an apprentice machinist in the city of Detroit.

Wilber [April 16, 1867—May 30, 1912] *and Orville* [August 19, 1871—January 30, 1948] *Wright,* were two Americans who are generally credited with inventing and building the world's first successful airplane and making the first controlled, powered and sustained heavier than air human flight, on December 17, 1903. They are also officially credited worldwide through the Fédération Aéronautique Internationale, the standard-setting and record keeping body for aeronautics and astronautics, as "the first sustained and controlled heavier-than-air powered flight." In the two years afterward, the brothers developed their flying machine into the first practical fixed-wing aircraft. Although not the first to build and fly experimental aircraft, the Wright brothers were the first to invent aircraft controls that made fixed wing flight possible.

The brothers' fundamental breakthrough was their invention of three-axis control, which enabled the pilot to steer the aircraft effectively and to maintain its equilibrium. This method became standard and remains standard on fixed wing aircraft of all kinds. From the beginning of their aeronautical work, the Wright brothers focused on unlocking the secrets of control to conquer "the flying problem," rather than developing more powerful engines as some other experimenters did. Their careful wine tunnel tests produced better aeronautical data than any before, enabling them to design and build wings and propellers more effective than any before. Their U.S. Patent 821,393 claims the invention of a system of aerodynamic control that manipulates a flying machine surfaces.

They gained the mechanical skills essential for their success by working for years in their shop with printing presses, bicycles, motors, and other machinery. Their work with bicycles in particular influenced their belief that an unstable vehicle like a flying machine could be controlled and balanced with practice. From 1900 until their first powered flights in late 1903, they conducted extensive glider tests that also developed their skills as pilots. Their bicycle shop employee Charlie Taylor became an important part of the team, building their first aircraft engine in close collaboration with the brothers.

Steve Wozniak [born August 11, 1950 in San Jose, California] is an American computer engineer who founded

Apple Computer, Inc. (now Apple, Inc.) with Steve Jobs. His inventions and machines are credited with contributing significantly to the personal computer revolution of the 1970s. Wozniak created the Apple I and Apple II computers in the mid-1970s. In the movie *"Pirates of Silicon Valley,"* it depicts him as actually the principle source of what we know as *Microsoft Windows*. The Apple II gained much popularity, eventually becoming one of the best selling personal computers of *the 1970s and early 1980a.*

William Henry "Bill" Gates III [born October 28, 1955] is an American business magnate, philanthropist, author, and chairman of Microsoft, the software company he founded with Paul Allen. He is ranked consistently one of the world's wealthiest people and the wealthiest overall as of 2009. During his career at Microsoft, Gates held the position of CEO and chief software architect, and remains the largest individual shareholder with more than 8 percent of the common stock. He has also authored or co-authored several books.

Gates is one of the best-known entrepreneurs of the personal computer revolution. Although many admire him, a number of industry insiders criticize his business tactics, which they consider anti-competitive, an opinion that has in some cases been upheld by the courts. In later stages of his career, Gates pursued a number of philanthropic endeavors, donating large amounts of money to various charitable organizations and scientific research programs through the Bill & Melinda Gates Foundation, established in 2000.

Alexander Graham Bell [3 March 1847—2 August 1922] was an eminent scientist, inventor, engineer and innovator who is credited with inventing the first practical telephone.

Bell's father, grandfather, and brother had all been associated with work on elocution and speech, and both his mother and wife were deaf, profoundly influencing Bell's life's work. His research on hearing and speech further led him to experiment with hearing devices, which eventually culminated in Bell being awarded the first U.S. patent for the telephone in 1876. In retrospect, Bell considered his most famous invention an intrusion on his real work as a scientist and refused to have a telephone in his study.

Many other inventions marked Bell's later life, including groundbreaking work in hydrofoils and aeronautics. In 1888, Alexander Graham Bell became one of the founding members of the National Geographic Society.

Thomas Jefferson: said: "I have examined all the known superstitions of the world, and I do not find in our particular superstition of Christianity one redeeming feature. They are all alike founded on fables and mythology. Millions of innocent men, women and children, since the introduction of Christianity, have been burnt, tortured, fined and imprisoned. What has been the effect of all this coercion? To make one half the world fools and the other half hypocrites; to support roguery and error all over the earth." He also said, "Christianity is the most perverted system that ever shone on man." (Page 43, "The God Delusion," by Richard Dawkins). Also, he said, "A professorship of theology should have no place in our institution." (Page 75 in Dawkins). Jefferson also said: "To talk of immaterial existences is to talk of *nothings*. To say that the human soul, angels, god, are immaterial, is to say they are nothings, or that there is no god, no angels, no souls. I cannot reason otherwise…without plunging into the fathomless abyss of dreams and phantasms. I am satisfied, and sufficiently occupied with the things which are, without tormenting myself about those which may indeed be, but of which I have no evidence." He also wrote to his nephew Peter Carr: "Shake off all the fears of servile prejudices, under which weak minds are servilely crouched. Fix reason firmly in her seat, and call on her tribunal for every fact, every opinion. Question with boldness even the existence of a God; because, if there be one, he must more approve of the homage of reason than that of blindfolded fear." Thomas Jefferson was an enlightenment thinker. His nemesis Alexander Hamilton paid him an extremely high compliment by throwing all the support he could of the Federalist Party to him rather than Aaron Burr because whatever else Jefferson was "Jefferson was incorruptible." **Jefferson** took everything supernatural, i.e., all miracles, out of the "Jefferson Bible." After Jefferson was finished modifying the "Jefferson Bible," it has less that 1% of the words of the original Bible. Thomas Jefferson wrote the Declaration of Independence. He was the third president of the United States. He was a scientist and a lover of science. He was the leading U.S. scientist in various fields. He was an inventor and the very first Patent Examiner in the first Constitutional Patent System on earth. He is recognized as the greatest democratic philosopher of all time. But, He is most recognized for his politics. He actually was the author of most of the characteristics of the United States that made it the wonderful place it is or at least used to be. Jefferson's one serious mistake was that he thought the U.S. citizens would, through education, reject Christianity and become deist, like himself, or Unitarian Universalist, like some thought he was. Incidentally, Jefferson wrote the Declaration of

Independence before *Antoine Lavoisier's* work back in 1778, and did not know about the *Law of Conservation of Mass or Energy* during his education years. He also lived before Charles Darwin. Jefferson like Washington, Adams, Madison and Monroe had no religious person at his bedside when he

died. *Jefferson's recitation of the dogmas of Calvin:*
1. *That there are three Gods.*
2. *That good works, or the love of our neighbor, is nothing.*
3. *That faith is every thing, and the more incomprehensible the proposition, the more merit the faith.*
4. *That reason in religion is of unlawful use.*
5. *That God, from the beginning, elected certain individuals to be saved, and certain others to be damned; and that no crimes of the former can damn them; no virtues of the latter save."*
--To Benjamin Waterhouse, Jun. 26, 1822

Thomas Paine, the pamphleteer who almost certainly had more to do with our winning the American Revolution than anyone except Washington, himself, and the greatest Democratic visionary than anyone except Jefferson himself, said, "Of all the **tyrannies** that affect mankind, **tyranny in religion** is the worst."(Bold face added) He also said: "The New Testament, they tell us, is founded upon the prophecies of the Old; if so, it must follow the fate of its foundation." He further said: "Whenever we read the obscene stories, the voluptuous debaucheries, the cruel and torturous executions, the unrelenting vindictiveness, with which more than half of the Bible is filled, it would be more consistent that we call it the word of a demon than the word of God. It is a history of wickedness that has served to corrupt and brutalize mankind." He also wrote The *Age of Reason*, which totally rejects Christianity in emphatic terms. He also said:

"The Christian religion is a parody on the worship of the sun, in which they put a man called Christ in the place of the sun, and pay him the adoration originally payed to the sun."

Abraham Lincoln, although not a Founding Father, was an extremely influential and important U.S. President. He is considered, after George Washington, the greatest of presidents. Every child is taught about Lincoln's birth in a log cabin, but what is not taught is that he rejected Christianity, never joined a church, and even wrote a treatise against religion. At times religious wording was written into Lincoln's speeches, but such public soothes were brought at the insistence of White House staff members. (Actually the Lincoln staff's first insertion of "Under God" into Lincoln's Gettysburg Address was, I believe, the first crack Christians were able to drive into Jefferson's sacred *Wall of Separation Between Church and State*, and I think it was added after his death because it wasn't in the script of the speech. We shouldn't let Christians do such things because now they are taking the entire country). In 1843, after he lost a campaign for Congress, he wrote to his supporters: "It was everywhere contended no Christian ought to vote for me because I belonged to no church, and was suspected of being a Deist." When Lincoln was first considered for the presidential nomination, Logan Hay wrote to his nephew, the future Secretary of State John Hay: "Candor compels me to say that Mr. Lincoln could hardly be termed a devout believer in the authenticity of the Bible (but this is for your ears only)." Interviewer Opie Read once asked Lincoln about his conception of God, to which he replied: "The same as my conception of nature." When he was asked what he meant by that, he said: "That it is impossible for either to be personal." His former law partner, William Herndon, said of him after his assassination: "[Mr. Lincoln] never mentioned the name

of Jesus, except to scorn and detest the idea of a miraculous conception. He did write a little work on infidelity in 1835-6, and never recanted. He was an out-and-out infidel, and about that there is no mistake." He also said that Lincoln "assimilated into his own being" the heretical book *Age of Reason* by Thomas Paine. Lincoln's first law partner, John T. Stuart, said of him: "He was an open infidel, and sometimes bordered on atheism. He went further against Christian beliefs and doctrines and principles than any man I have ever heard." He also said: "The Bible is not my book nor Christianity my profession. I could never assent to the long, complicated statements of Christian dogma."

*"The returning good sense of our country threatens abortion to their hopes, & they [the clergy] believe that any portion of power confided to me, will be exerted in opposition to their schemes. And they believe rightly; for **I have sworn upon the alter of God, eternal hostility against every form of tyranny over the mind of man**"[bold face added]—*
Thomas Jefferson—

Chapter V

People And Institutions Who Take Advantage Of Our Fundamental Training To Believe Lies Despite Evidence

The Constitutional basis: Article I

Section 8. The Congress shall have power To borrow money on the credit of the United States…To coin money, regulate the value thereof, and of foreign coin… To raise and support armies, but no appropriation of money to that use shall be for a longer term than two years…To declare war…

So who wants to take the Roman Tyrants place in benefiting tremendously from the enslavement provided by the Christian Con Artist Industry? What has all this Christian indoctrination, "wonderful good" faith despite evidence, disinterest in science and technology and great interest in sports, movies, drugs, alcohol and other entertainment or distractions been preparing us for?

As made clear from Chapter II, they must have been preparing us to be somebody's slaves. To find out let's take a look at the third and second parts of Zeitgeist the movie and G. Edward Griffin's *"The Creature From Jeckyl Island."*

Americans [and the rest of the world] have been totally conned by the Con Artists of the Federal Reserve System [and other privately owned and controlled central banks of the world].

At one time the American Colonies actually had an honest monetary system, but King George III sought to destroy this honest monetary system, which was a primary reason for the American Revolution:

"The refusal of King George III to allow the colonies to operate an honest money system, which freed the ordinary man from the clutches of the money manipulators was probably the prime cause of the revolution."—Benjamin Franklin

Down thru time many people have warned us about central banks:

"There is something behind the throne greater than the King himself."—Sir William Pitt—House of Lords 1770

"The world is governed by very different personages from what is imagined by those who are not behind the scenes."—Benjamin Dislaeli—English Statesman 1844

King George III of Great Britain outlawed the interest free independent currency the colonies were producing themselves. In turn forcing them to borrow money from the central bank of England at interest. Immediately putting the colonies into debt.

In 1783 America won its independence from England; however, its battle against the central bank concept and the corrupt, greed filled, and ruthless con artists associated with it had just begun.

So why are Central Banks so bad? When the bankers explain Central Banking, they take a relatively simple concept and by the time they finish *"explaining it,"* we have no idea what they are talking about. In other words they use *"smoke and mirror"* language.

The Federal Reserve System is *"an appearance that is not, but yet appears to be,"* i.e., *loaded with deception.*

If there is anything in the world that has a deceiving appearance, it is the Federal Reserve System.

In plain English, what is a Central Bank?

The Central Bank is an institution that produces the entire currency of a nation. Three powers are inherent in central banking practice:

1. Control of Interest Rates.
2. Creation of money at interest from nothing,
3. Control of Inflation [money supply, i.e., debt].
   a. Whether the small people's Banks have power to Loan out a large amount of Money, or
   b. Whether the small people's Banks are forced to call in all their loans to cause foreclosures that cause panics or depressions in order for Central Bankers to steal trillions of dollars from Americans by buying multiple Banks

and Corporations at pennies on the dollar.

The Central Bank does not simply supply a government's economy with money. It unconstitutionally loans it to them at interest.

Money is debt under the Federal Reserve Act. Debt is money under the Federal Reserve Act.

"If there were no debt in our money system, there wouldn't be any money."—Marriner Eccles (1890-1977)—while Chairman and Governor of the Federal Reserve Board—In office (1934-1948) during the Franklin Roosevelt and Harry Truman administrations.

If one were to make a graph of the United States money supply it would be virtually identical to a graph of the United States National debt under the Federal Reserve Act.

Then with the use of increasing and decreasing the supply of money the Central Bank regulates the value of the currency being issued. It is critical to understand that the entire structure of this system can lead to only one thing in the long run: debt.

Every single dollar of this system is loaned at interest. This means every single dollar produced is:

1 DOLLAR
+
"X" percent of this dollar in immediate debt

Since the Central Bank has a monopoly of the entire production of money at interest of the entire country, and they unconstitutionally loan each dollar out with immediate debt attached to it, where does the money to pay the debt come from? It can only come from the Central Bank again.

This means the Central Bank has to perpetually increase its money supply [debt] to temporarily cover the outstanding debt created. Which in turn, since that new money is loaned out at interest as well creates even more debt.

The end result of this without fail is slavery.

Debt = Slavery

It is impossible for the government and the people to ever come out of this unconstitutional self generated debt. These Central Bankers are actually golden tongue thieves.

It doesn't take a lot of ingenuity to figure this scam out. The central bank has to perpetually increase its money supply [debt] to temporarily cover the outstanding debt created, which in turn, since that new money is loaned out at interest as well, creates even more debt. The end result of this system without fail is slavery.

The founding fathers were well aware of this. Thomas Jefferson, the greatest Democratic visionary and friend America ever had said:

"If the American People ever allow the banks to control the issuance of their currency, first by inflation and then by deflation, the banks and corporations that will grow up around them will deprive the people of all their property, until their children will wake up homeless on the continent their fathers occupied. The issuing of money should be taken from the banks and restored to Congress and the people to

whom it belongs." –Thomas Jefferson

George Washington's Secretary of Treasury and Jefferson's nemesis, Alexander Hamilton, lobbied for the first privately owned Federal Bank, and in 1789 Congress chartered the bank for 20 years.

Twenty years later in 1809 Jefferson refused to renew its charter, saying:

"I sincerely believe the banking institutions having the issuing power of money are more dangerous to liberty than standing armies."—Thomas Jefferson

Note here that we [and many in the rest of the world] now have both standing armies and central banks, i.e., thieves of our lives, liberty and wealth fully empowered.

A British man: said:

"If you want to remain slaves of the bankers and pay for the cost of your own slavery, let them contrive to create money and control the nations' credit."—Sir Josia Stamp [1880-1941],

The second Federal Bank [a privately owned central bank like our Fed] was established in 1816 in James Madison's administration. Andrew Jackson closed the second Federal Bank in 1836 with these comments to congress before revoking its charter:

"Gentlemen, I have had men watching you for a long time and I am convinced that you have used the funds of the bank to speculate in the breadstuffs of the country. When you won, you divided the profits amongst you, and when you

lost you charged it to the bank. You tell me that if I take the deposits from the bank and annul its charter, I shall ruin ten thousand families. That may be true, gentlemen, but that is your sin! Should I let you go on, you will ruin fifty thousand families, and that would be my sin! You are a den of vipers and thieves. "—Andrew Jackson {1767-1845)

After revoking the central bank's charter, Jackson told the congress:

"If Congress has the right under the Constitution to issue paper money, it was given to be used by themselves, not to be delegated to individuals or corporations. "—Andrew Jackson (1767-1845)

Abraham Lincoln weighed in later:
"The Government should create, issue, and circulate the currency and credits needed to satisfy the spending power of the Government and the buying power of the consumers. By the adoption of these principles, the taxpayers will be saved immense sums of interest. Money will cease to be the master and become the servant of humanity. "—Abraham Lincoln (1809-1865)

One thing Lincoln was saying was that money should not be issued as a loan at interest. In other words money should not be debt and we should have an honest money system such as we had almost continuously until 1913.

So, are four of the greatest Americans and intellectual giants of all time: Thomas Jefferson, Benjamin Franklin, Abraham Lincoln and Andrew Jackson wrong or right? Is the Fed as bad as they said? I say it certainly is that and worse.

[We had honest money for 163 years [1750-1913] except the first Fed 1789-1809 and the second Fed 1816-1836. This enabled recovery from the damage done by the

corrupt Fed before 1913.
    The *third time is the curse!*

By early 20th century the conspirators had already implemented and removed two central banking systems, which were swindled [or conned] into place by ruthless, golden tongue con artist banking interests.

At this time the dominant families in the banking business world were the Rockefellers, the Morgans, the Warburgs, and the ***Rothschilds.***

In the early 1900s they sought to push, once again, legislation to create another [third] central bank.

However, they knew the government and public were very wary of such an institution [back then people had a much more honest, truthful education than we now have].

So, they needed to create an incident [just like the bad guys in the old western movies of the 1930s till the 1960s, i.e., *"Old San Francisco"* with John Wayne and Albert Decker comes to mind] to affect public opinion.

J.P. Morgan, probably considered a financial luminary at the time, exploited his mass influence by publishing rumors that a prominent bank in New York was insolvent or bankrupt.

Morgan knew this would cause mass hysteria, which would affect other banks as well and, it did. The public, in fear of loosing their deposits, immediately began mass withdrawals.

Consequently, the banks were forced to call in their

loans, causing recipients to sell their property and thus a spiral of bankruptcies, repositions and turmoil emerged. Putting the pieces together a few years later Frederick Allen of Life Magazine wrote:

"The Morgan interests took advantage...to precipitate the panic of 1907, guiding it shrewdly as it progressed."— Frederick Allen—Life Magazine.

Unaware of the fraud, the panic of 1907 led to a congressional investigation headed by the con artist Senator Nelson Aldrich who had intimate ties to the banking cartels and later became part of the Rockefeller family thru marriage—Remember Gerald Ford's Vice-President: Nelson Aldrich Rockefeller his grandson—this indicates where the *"Liberals"* really came from.

The commission, lead by Aldrich recommended a central bank should be implemented *"so a panic like 1907 could never happen again."* This was the spark [or con artistry], the international banker con artists needed to initiate their plan.

In 1910 a super secret meeting was held at the Magnificent Estate, *"Club House,"* owned by J.P. Morgan and other millionaires from New York on Jeckyl Island off the coast of Georgia. It was there the central banking bill called the Federal Reserve Act was written. Bankers not lawmakers wrote this legislation.

This *"Club House,"* has been purchased by the state of Georgia. You can visit the *"Club House,"* take the tour and visit the room where the Federal Reserve System was created.

On the door entering that room is a plaque stating *the Federal Reserve System was created in this room.*

So this part of it is now public record, but for many years after the meeting nobody knew about it and each member denied it ever happened until well after the establishment of the Federal Reserve System.

In *"The Creature from Jeckyll Island"* by G. Edward Griffin, it states the Fed is a Cartel. This book gives an excellent description of the international banking cartels leading the world into serfdom. This is a must read book. It can also be obtained on DVD, CD, and watched on U-Tube.

What is a cartel? A Webster's dictionary definition of a cartel is "**2:** a combination of independent commercial enterprises designed to limit competition."

This meeting was so secretive and so concealed from government and public knowledge the seven figures that attended disguised their names when in route to the island.

Why the secrecy? It was a take over of the government of the United States by the richest of men who owned about a quarter of all the worlds wealth at the time of the take over.

They were cutthroat competitors before this act, but were a cooperating cutthroat monopoly after the act in partnership with the government and other banks to basically rob the American people of their wealth, which they have been doing ever since 1913.

After this bill was constructed, the bankers then handed it over to their political front con man Nelson Aldrich to push thru congress and in 1913 with heavy political [and banking cartel] sponsorship, Woodrow Wilson became president.

Having already agreed to sign this Federal Reserve Act in exchange for campaign support and two days before Christmas when most of congress was home with their families, the Federal Reserve Act was voted in and Wilson in turn made it law.

The 1913 swindling [or coning] of Woodrow Wilson into signing into law the privately owned Central Banking System [the Federal Reserve System] was later deeply regretted by Wilson. As evidence of this, Wilson stated:

"I am a most unhappy man. I have unwittingly ruined my country. A great industrial nation is controlled by a system of credit. Our system of credit is concentrated. The growth of the nation, therefore, and all our activities are in the hands of a few men. We have come to be one of the worst ruled, one of the most completely controlled and dominated governments in the civilized world – no longer a government by free opinion, no longer a government by conviction and the vote of the majority, but a government by the opinion and duress of a small group of dominant men."—Woodrow Wilson

Congressman Lewis McFadden also expressed the truth after the passage of the bill:
'A World Banking System is being set up here ...a super state controlled by international bankers ...acting together to enslave the world for their own pleasure, the Fed has usurped the Government."—Lewis McFadden

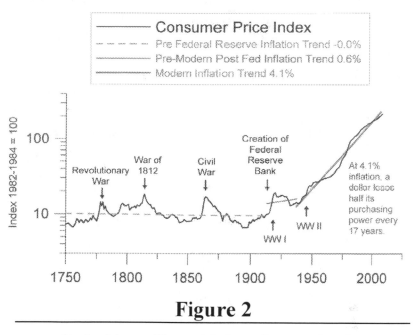

Figure 2

By looking at Figure 2 it is easily seen that the currency of the United States was holding its value from 1750 – 1913. For 163 years a dollar remained virtually a dollar, i.e., sometimes it had more purchasing power than average and sometimes less, but the purchasing power of the dollar averaged $1.00. But beginning in 1913-2007 after 94 years each quarter lost 24 cents in value [purchasing power] and in 2007 a quarter would buy only one cent of true value such as the original value of a dollar backed by gold. If one made an accurate graph of the average national debt, it would look flat, i.e., near zero, until 1913 and start going up astronomically after the installation of the Federal Reserve System installed in 1913. The Federal Reserve Act has robbed the wealth of the United States from us. It should be obvious from looking at Figures 2, 3 and 4 that America will become serfdom if we don't get rid of the Federal Reserve System. If we didn't have the Fed; still had honest currency, had a free Jeffersonian-Adam Smith [read Milton Freedman's *"Free to Choose"*] way of life and economy, and our patent system was working as our founders intended, we would still be the most powerful, prosperous and free industrial nation with by far the greatest life, liberty, happiness and wealth per capita in the world. As it is we are becoming virtual slaves and will most likely be serfdom in less than 30 years. Our wealth and currency value are going down logarithmically and our debt is going up astronomically. Concisely put: the Fed is stealing our rightful wealth and prosperity from us. [Data from Economic Leads]

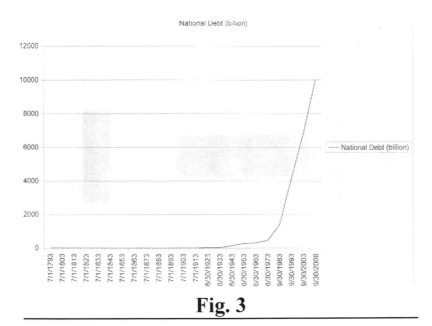

National Debt (billion)

Fig. 3

It can be seen from Figure 3 that the national debt did not start going up until after the establishment of the Federal Reserve System [December 1913] and it did not start to skyrocket until about 1973. [Data from Public Debt Historical Information archives]

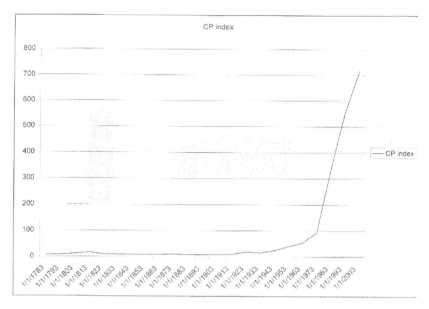

Fig. 4

It can be seen from Figures 3 and 4 that the linier graphs of the National Debt and the Consumer Price Index are virtually identical as would be a graph of the money supply [This could be easily shown if one had honest data of the money supply going back to 1783, 1793 or 1750]. Note: the CP index (Fig 4) starts in 1783 while the National Debt starts in 1793. Note: also Fig. 2 is on Simi log format while Fig. 3 and Fig. 4 are on linear format. [Data from Office of National Statistics]

Looking at Figures 2,3 and 4, it does not take a rocket scientist to see that America will become a serfdom if it does not make drastic changes, i.e., get rid of the Fed, all the false [red herring] economic theories and get back to Jeffersonian-Adam Smith free-enterprise economics with an honest government acting as an honest umpire to keep out the various excesses that sometimes arise in this system.

This free-enterprise system includes the principles of the Declaration of Independence: *WE hold these Truths to be self-evident, that all Men are created equal, that they are endowed by their Creator with certain unalienable Rights, that among these are Life, Liberty, and the Pursuit of Happiness—That to secure these Rights, Governments are instituted among Men, deriving their just Powers from the Consent of the Governed, that whenever any Form of Government becomes destructive to these Ends, it is the Right of the People to alter or to abolish it, and to institute new Government, laying its Foundation on such Principles, and organizing its Powers in such Form, as to them shall seem most likely to effect their Safety and Happiness.*

This system [*free enterprise*] is not perfect, but it is astronomically better than any other system, e.g., socialism, communism, fascism, or welfare state, ever tried, and people are infinitely more free and prosperous when true free enterprise exists without the serfdom lords, i.e., the Central Bank Cartels.

It should go without saying that this "*free enterprise system*" is certainly better to go back to than some totally untried system of totally unknown performance.

No matter what system is in place each person in the system is always trying [no matter what they will admit] to improve their own position, the position of their children, and the position of their grand children. That is the nature of a human being.

We are all human beings. The only system that truly works with the nature of human beings is *Jeffersonian free enterprise*. All other systems try to change human nature by force, deception or lies. This simply cannot be done. It simply results in tyranny and poverty.

The public was told [and is still being told] that the Federal Reserve System [cartel] was [is] an economic stabilizer and inflation and economic crises was [is] a thing of the past.

Well, as history [if one really looks at it] has shown [look at Figures 2, 3 and 4 above], nothing is further from the truth. We have been [and are being] lied to, big time!

The central bankers know how to streamline and machine to expand their personal ambitions. For example in 1914-1919 the Fed increased their money supply by about 100% resulting in extensive loans to small banks and the public.

Then in 1920 the Fed called in mass percentages of the outstanding money supply thus forcing the supporting banks to call in huge numbers of loans and just like 1907 bank runs, bankruptcies and huge collapses occurred over 5400 public banks outside the Federal Reserve System collapsed further consolidating the already small group of international bankers.

Privy to this crime Congressman Lindberg stepped up and said:

"Under the Federal Reserve Act, Panics are scientifically created. The present panic is the first scientifically created one, worked out as we figure a mathematical equation."—Charles Lindberg

However, the Panic of 1920 was just a warm up. From 1920 - 1929, the Fed again increased the money supply

62% resulting once again in extensive loans to the public and banks.

There was also a fairly new kind of loan called a margin loan in the stock market. Very simply the margin loan allowed an investor to put down only 10% of his investment to get 100% control of his stock's price with the other 90% being loaned by someone, such as the broker.

In other words a person could own $1000 worth of stock with only $100 down. This method was very popular in the roaring 1920s and everyone seemed to be making money in the market.

However, there is a catch to this loan. It could be called in at any time and had to be paid within 24 hours. This is termed a margin call. [a 24 hour margin call could occur at any time]

The typical result of a margin call is the selling of the stock purchased with the loan.

So, a few months before October in 1929, J.D. Rockefeller, Bernard Barrack and others quietly exited the market and on October 24th 1929, the New York Financiers who financed the margin loans started calling them in mass.

This sparked an instantaneous massive sell off in the market because everyone had to cover their margin calls.

Eventually the mass bank loans were called in for the same reason causing the collapse of some 16000 banks enabling international bankers, at discounts, to not only buy up small banks but whole corporations at pennies on the dollar.

It was one of the greatest thefts of our liberty, happiness and wealth in American history. [Another crime our Lords the Banking Cartel got away with.]

Rather than expanding the money supply to reduce the unemployment and difficulties of the American citizens, **the Fed actually contracted the money supply on purpose**.

They thereby fueled the worst depression in our history on purpose to enrich themselves and bring America to its knees.

In 1931, serfdom's Trojan Horse, Franklin D. Roosevelt was elected into the presidency. Rather than blame the true villain: the Federal Reserve System, Roosevelt, and the news media blamed free enterprise and capitalism and ignored the warnings and precedents of the giants: Jefferson, Franklin, Lincoln and Jackson.

Roosevelt and his press set forth all kinds of red herrings as cures, i.e., Keynesian economics, Socialism, Communism, Liberalism, a Welfare State etc.

Let us face it; by far the most successful economic system in the history of the world is the *Jeffersonian-Adam Smith free enterprise system*. We just need a government that acts as a referee to eternally stop the plunderers of it such as our Lords the Federal Reserve System.

Once again outraged congressman Lewis McFadden, a long time opponent of our Lords the central bankers and international cartels, began bringing impeachment proceedings against the Federal Reserve Board. Saying of the event:

"It was a carefully contrived occurrence. International Bankers sought to bring about a condition of despair so that they might emerge the rulers of us all."— Lewis McFadden

Not surprisingly and after two former assassination attempts, **McFadden was poisoned** at a banquet before he could push for the impeachment. *[Another crime our Lords the Fed Cartel got away with.]*

Now having reduced the society to squallier the Federal Reserve Cartel decided that the Gold Standard should be removed

In order to do this they needed to acquire the remaining gold in the system. Selling of the gold under the pretense of helping terminate the depression came in the 1933 gold seizure. [Another crime our Lords the Fed Cartel got away with]

Under the threat of imprisonment for ten years, everyone in America was required to turn in all gold bullions etc. to the treasury. Essentially robbing the public of what little wealth they had left.

At the end of 1933, the gold standard was abolished.

If you look at a dollar bill issued before 1933, it says it is redeemable in gold. *[Also it does not say "In God We Trust"].*

If you look at a dollar bill today, it says it is legal tender, which is backed by absolutely nothing *[but now it says "In God We Trust"].* It is worthless paper.

The only thing that gives our money value is the psychological effect of how much of it is in circulation.

Therefore, the power to regulate the money supply is also the power to regulate its value, which is also the power to bring entire economies and societies to its knees.

"Let me issue and control a nation's money and I care not who makes its laws."—Mayer Amschel Rothschild [1744-1812], Founder of the Rothschild Dynasty

"History records that the money changers have used every form of abuse, intrigue, deceit, and violent means possible to maintain their control over governments by controlling money and its issuance."—James Madison, 4th U.S. President and Father of the U.S. Constitution

If one stops to think, this means the Federal Reserve System is empowered to and does print multitrillions of dollars from nothing except paper that bring them multitrillions of dollars in interest income for virtually no service rendered, except the printing of the virtually costless paper money, at trillions of dollars in interest lost by the taxpayers of the United States.

If one thinks further the smaller banks of the U.S. can create nine times that much money by keeping 10% of the money and loaning out 90% of the money created by the Fed from nothing except virtually costless paper.

The Constitutional way: Constitutional money is gold or silver. Originally these precious metals were sent to owners of the mint and transformed into coins. This money was then spent into the economy and remained in circulation.

No inflation [or actual devaluation of the dollar] resulted.

Every dollar improved the economy of the country, and in an exchange of goods or services for money, the seller received true value in gold or silver, or in gold or silver certificates.

Even if Congress were to issue debt money, the interest would be returned to the U.S. Treasury, not to a *private* bank controlled by international bankers.

What we now have is actually a tax that doesn't cover government expense and must be paid for by taxpayers. It only enriches our Lords, the ruthless, greedy owners of the Federal Reserve System [Cartel] at taxpayer expense.

No wonder the national debt; money supply and inflation have gone upward through the roof!

It is important to clearly understand. The Federal Reserve is a private Corporation that functions as a Cartel. It is about as Federal as Federal Express.

Lewis vs. U.S., 608F 2d 1239 (1982)—Mr. Lewis was injured by a Federal Reserve vehicle and sued the U.S. government. On April 17, 1982, the court ruled: "*...that since the Federal Reserve System and its twelve branch banks are private corporations, the federal government could not be held responsible.*"

It is a Private Corporation.
It functions as a Cartel
It makes its own policies.
It is under virtually no regulation by the U.S. government.

It is a private bank that loans all the currency at interest.

It is the fraudulent corrupt monetary system that the U.S. government and people tried to escape from by fighting the American Revolution.

It is even worse now. In 1965, under President Johnson, silver was removed from our coins. And in 1978, during the Carter administration, Congress took us off the remaining gold standard that still existed. The American people and their descendents were robbed and did nothing.

What is worse the Fed has addicted Congress. Because, since our currency is not backed by gold or silver, Congress can spend all it wants knowing full well that the Fed will eagerly provide them with the money at interest to the taxpayer.

They will not have to raise taxes—they just unconstitutionally put us deeper and deeper in debt. We are paying more and more interest and congressmen and congresswomen are getting richer and richer at taxpayer expense!

Who do the people of the Fed actually work for? Although the president appoints members of the Federal Reserve Board of governors, their 14-year terms mean they can outlast presidential influences.

Federal Reserve workers are not civil service employees.

In *"Secrets of the Federal Reserve,"* Eustace Mullins states that the principle shareholders of the Fed are:

the Rothschilds, Lazard Feres, Israel Schiff, Kuhn-Loeb
Co., Warburg Co., Lehman Brothers, Goldman-Sachs, the
Rockefeller family, and the J.P. Morgan interests. To whom
do you think the Fed owe its allegiance?

To sum things up: on December 23, 1913, Congress
passed the Federal Reserve Act resulting in ***the greatest
theft in the history of the world!*** Ultimately causing a U.S.
Federal debt to rise from virtually nothing to over ten trillion
dollars [$10,000,000,000,000] in 2009, the loss of America's
gold and silver reserves, the devastation of the U.S. economy
and most of the great American economic principles such as a
well functioning U.S. Patent System, i.e., promoting progress
in "science and useful arts."

Going back to 1913, the Federal Reserve Act was not
the only unconstitutional Bill pushed through Congress.

They also pushed the Federal Income Tax. It is
worthwhile to point out that the public's ignorance toward the
Federal Income Tax is a testament to how dumbed down and
oblivious the American public really is.

And of how little help the U.S. Press really was at that
time [and is now].

First of all the Federal Income Tax is completely
unconstitutional. It is a direct unapportioned tax. All Federal
taxes have to be apportioned to be legal according to the U.S.
Constitution.

Second, the required number of states was never met.
It was not properly ratified. This has been cited by modern
judges:

"I think if you were to go back and try to find and review the ratification of the 16th amendment, which was the Internal Revenue, Income Tax. I think if you went back and examined that carefully, you would find that a sufficient number of states never ratified that amendment"—U.S. District Court Judge James C. Fox 2003

But he did say he didn't think any court would set it aside because it has not been contested over such a long period of time. This is because the American press and the dumbed down public failed to do their job.

Third, at the present day roughly 25% of the average worker's income is taken by this tax, and guess where that money goes.

It goes to pay the interest on the money being printed by the fraudulent Federal Reserve Bank; *a system that does not have to exist at all*.

And a system we must stop if we don't want to become serfdom.

So, the earnings of average workers for some three months out of the year go into the pockets of the private international bankers who own the Federal Reserve Banking Cartel.

Fourth, even with the fraudulent government claim as to the legality of the Income Tax, there is literally no statute; no law exists that requires you to pay this tax.

Income Tax Is

1. **Unconstitutional**
2. **The Income Tax Amendment was not ever ratified.**
3. **Nearly all the tax goes to the Federal Banking Cartel.**
4. **No Statute or Law Exist for the Income Tax**

IRS agents have looked for that law and have been totally unable to find it, i.e. ex IRS agents--Joe Turner and Sherry Jackson. The Income Tax is nothing less than the enslavement of the entire country.

However, as Judge Fox said or implied, these unlawful acts have not been contested over such a long period that the courts probably can't invalidate them now.

The control of the economy and the perpetual robbery of wealth is only one side of the rubrics cube the bankers hold in their hands. The next tool for profit and control is war.

Since the inception of the Federal Reserve of 1913, a number of large and small wars have commenced. The five most pronounced were:

1. World War I,
2. World War II,
3. Vietnam,
4. Iraq and
5. Afghanistan.

World War I; in 1914 European wars broke out centered around England and Germany. The American public wanted nothing to do with the war. In turn President Wilson publicly declared neutrality.

However, under the surface the Wilson administration was looking for any excuse they could find to enter the war.

"The large banking interest were deeply interested in the World War because of the wide opportunities for large profits"—said William Jennings Bryan

It is important to understand that the most lucrative thing that can happen for the central bankers is war for it forces the country to barrow even more money from the Federal Reserve Banking Cartel at interest.

Woodrow Wilson's top adviser and mentor was Colonel Edward House, a man with intimate connection with the International Banking Cartels who wanted us in the war. [I wonder if an international banker con artist has been behind the electing of each president since Wilson].

In a documented conversation between Colonel Edward House and Sir Edward Grey, the Foreign Secretary of England, regarding how to get America into the war,

Grey inquired: *"What will Americans do if Germans sink an ocean liner with American passengers on board?"*

House responded: *"I believe that a flame of indignation would sweep the United States and that by itself would be sufficient to carry us into war."*

So, on May 7, 1915, on essentially the suggestion of Sir Edward Grey, a ship called the Lusitanian was deliberately sent into German controlled waters where

German controlled vessels were known to be and as expected German U-Boats torpedoed the ship, exploded stored explosives and killed 1260 people.

To further understand the deliberate nature of this set up, the German Embassy actually put advertisements in the New York Times telling people that if they boarded the Lusitanian, they did so at their own peril. One advertisement said:

"NOTICE

TRAVELERS intending to embark on the Atlantic voyage are reminded that a state of war exists between Germany and her allies and Britain and her allies; that the zone of war includes the waters adjacent to the British Isles; that in accordance with formal notice given by the Imperial German Government, Vessels flying the flag of Great Britain or of any of her allies are liable to destruction in these waters and that travelers sailing in the war zone on ships of Great Britain or her allies do so at their own risk."—Imperial German Embassy

In turn and as anticipated the sinking of the Lusitanian caused a wave of anger within the American public and America entered the war a short time afterwards.

The First World War cost 320,512 dead and wounded Americans. But the central bankers, our masters, only cared about the money they made [stole] at taxpayers expense and other benefits they received. Nothing else.

John D, Rockefeller made $200 million from this war back when a dollar was almost a dollar rather than 1/25th of a dollar as was the case in, 2007. The war cost an estimated

$30 billion back when a dollar was worth almost a dollar.

Most of this was barrowed from the Federal Reserve Bank at interest to further the profits of the international bankers. See how the Fed rips money off the American people in direct defiance of Jefferson, Franklin, Jackson and Lincoln's best efforts to keep it from happening.

Wake up America! We can't let the Fed destroy our country! This was once the land of the free! It was once the greatest land in the world!

We must stop letting the Feds and their assistants destroy America. Who are the Feds assistants? They are many of the presidents, senators, congressmen, judicial members and our controlled press from Woodrow Wilson until now 2009! We have to stop them from destroying America!

World War II: On December 7, 1941, Japan attacked the American Fleet at Pearl Harbor triggering our entry into that war. President Franklin Roosevelt declared the day as "*a day that will live in infamy.*"

A day of infamy indeed, but not because of the alleged surprise attack on Pearl Harbor.

After 60 years of researching historical information, it has become extremely clear that not only was the attack known weeks in advance, but also, it was outright wanted and provoked [actually my mother told me this when I was a boy, but few believed it].

Roosevelt, whose family had been New York Bankers since the 18th century and whose uncle Frederick was on the original Federal Reserve Board, was very sympathetic with the interests of the international bankers [that are destroying America], and their interest was to enter the war.

As we have seen, nothing is more profitable for international bankers than war.

In a journal entry by Roosevelt's Secretary of War, Henry Stemson dated November 25, 1941; he documented a conversation he had with Roosevelt.

"The question was: how should we maneuver them into firing the first shot... It was desirable to make sure the Japanese be the ones to do this so that there should remain no doubt who were the aggressors"

Charles Lindberg, one of the greatest Americans of all time, himself tried hard to warn us saying:

"When hostilities commenced in Europe in 1939, it was realized that the American people had no intention of entering the war, but they believed that this country could be emplaced in the war in very much the same way that it was emplaced into the last war [World War I]. They planned first to prepare the United States for foreign war under the guise of American defense, second to involve us in the war step by step without our realization, third to create a series of incidents, which would force us into the actual conflict. These plans were to be planned and assisted by the full power of their propaganda. Our theaters soon became filled with our planes propagandizing the glory of war. Newsreels lost all semblance of objectivity, and they have used the war to justify restriction of congressional power and the assumption of dictatorial procedures on the part of the president and his appointees. A fear campaign was inaugurated. We cannot allow the natural passions and prejudices of other peoples

to lead our country to destruction. —Charles Lindberg
September 11, 1941.

In the months leading up to the attack on Pearl Harbor,
Roosevelt [in service to his Lords, the banking cartel]
had done almost everything within his power to anger the
Japanese showing a posture of aggression.

1. He halted all of Japan's imports of American
   Petroleum and all American goods.
2. He froze all the Japanese assets in the United
   States.
3. He made public loans to Nationalist China in
   support of their war efforts and applied military aid
   to the British, both enemies of Japan, which is in
   complete violation of international war rules.
4. On December 4, three days before the attack,
   Australians told him of a Japanese task force
   moving towards Pearl Harbor. Roosevelt ignored
   it.
5. So, as hoped and allowed on December 7, Japan
   attacked Pearl Harbor killing 2400 soldiers [one of
   them my cousin].

Actually, my mother told me this right after the war
started, but nobody else, that I knew of, believed it or would
believe it.

Before Pearl Harbor 83% of Americans wanted nothing
to do with the war. After Pearl Harbor one million men
volunteered for the war.

It is interesting, if one thinks about it, Serfdom's Trojan
Horse, Franklin Roosevelt did major things that converted
America from a Jeffersonian-Adam Smith free enterprise

system, which caused us to be the greatest country in the world, to a socialist-welfare-state type country basically ruled by our Lords the Fed, which is causing our downfall and Serfdom, i.e.,

1. He fully activated and empowered our Lords, the Federal Reserve Cartel to basically be our rulers.
2. He used the great depression the Fed caused to replace our great free enterprise system with his socialist-welfare-state type system.
3. He used World War II that he basically got us into to replace our free enterprise system with his socialist-welfare-state system.

Roosevelt reminds me of the golden tongue promoters: loading foolish children on the bus to *"Pleasure Island"* in Walt Disney's movie *"Pinocchio"* to become servile donkeys.

Americans jumped at the chance to jump aboard Roosevelt's vehicle to *"Pleasure Island."* Now we are all serfs to our Lords the international banking cartel and it is getting worse every year.

When a person watches a World War II movie such as *"Since You Went Away,"* with: Claudette Colbert, Shirley Temple, Jennifer Jones, Joseph Cotton, Robert Walker, Monty Wooly and Agnes Morehead, it is heartbreaking to realize how these wonderful, patriotic people sacrificed [some dieing in service to their country] primarily so the greedy banking cartels and their associates could make trillions off the American taxpayer.

It is important to note: Nazy Germany's war effort was largely supported by two organizations: one of which was called I.G. Farben. I.G. Farben produced 84% of Germany's explosives and Zuiclon B used in Concentration Camps to kill millions.

One of the unspoken partners of I.G. Farben was John D. Rockefeller's Standard Oil Company in America. In fact the German Air Force could not operate without a special additive patented by J.D. Rockefeller's Standard Oil Company.

The bombing of London by Germany, for example, was made possible by a $20 million sale of fuel to I.G. Farben by Rockefeller's Standard Oil Co. This is just one small point on the topic of how American Business funded both sides of World War II.

One other treasonous organization worth mentioning is the Union Banking Corporation of New York City. Not only did it finance numerous aspects to Hitler's rise to power along with actual materials during the war. It was also a Nazi money-laundering Bank. Which was eventually exposed for having millions of dollars of Nazi money in its vaults.

The Union Banking Company of New York was eventually seized for violations:

"[Vesting Order No. 248]

All the banking stock of Union Banking Corporation and certain indebtedness by it:

*Under the authority of **The Trading With The Enemy Act**, as amended, and Executive Order 9095, as amended, and pursuant to law the undersigned after investigation, finding:*

(a) That the property described as follows:
All of the Capital Stock of Union Banking Corporation,

*a New York Corporation, New York, New York which is
a business enterprise...* "

Guess who the President of the Union Bank was? It
was Prescott Bush, the father of George H.W. Bush and the
grandfather of George W. Bush. Keep that in mind while
considering the moral and political rectitude of the Bush
family who are notoriously unfriendly to the non-religious
secularists.

Vietnam: The United States official declaration of war
on Vietnam in 1964 came out of an alleged incident involving
two U.S. destroyers being attacked by North Vietnam P.T.
Boats in the Gulf of Tonkin. This was known as the Gulf
of Tonkin Incident. This single incident was the catalytic
pretence for massive troop deployment and full-fledged
warfare.

One problem, however, the attack on the U.S.
Destroyers by North Vietnamese P.T. Boats never happened.
It was a completely staged event. It was a completely staged
event used as an excuse to enter the war.

Former Secretary of Defense Robert McNamara stated
years later: "The Gulf of Tonkin was a Mistake." Many other
officers and insiders have come forward relaying that it was a
contrived farce; a complete lie.

Once in the War, it was business as usual. In October,
1966, President Lyndon Johnson lifted trading restrictions on
the Soviet Block while knowing full well the Soviets were
providing 80% of North Vietnam's war supplies.

Consequently Rockefeller interest financed factories
in the Soviet Union, which the Soviets used to manufacture

military equipment, which was used by the North Vietnamese; however, this was only one side of the coin.

In 1985 rules of engagement were declassified. This detailed what American Troops were and were not allowed to do in the war. It included absurdities like:

1. North Vietnamese Anti Missile Systems could not be bombed until they were known to be fully operational.
2. No enemy could be pursued into the surrounding areas [crossed the border of Laos or Cambodia]. And most revealing of all
3. The most critical strategic targets were not allowed to be engaged unless initiated by high officials only.

Apart from these imposed ludicrous limitations, North Vietnam was informed of these restrictions and therefore could base its entire strategies around them, the limitations of the American Forces.

This is why the War went on so long. The bottom line is this. The Vietnam War was never meant to be won. Just sustained. This war for profit resulted in 58,000 Americans dead and 3,000,000 Vietnamese dead.

Iraq and Afghanistan: So, where are we now? September 11, 2001, was jump-start for what are now an accelerated agenda by the ruthless cartels, i.e., international con artists. This was an inside job no different from

1. The sinking of the Lusitanian.
2. The provoking of the Pearl Harbor Attack
3. The staged Gulf of Tonkin Attack, and most

recently:

4. The intentional demolition, by demolition experts, of **3 World Trade Center towers** that were supposed to be **caused by two [2]** hijacked airplanes flown by "Terrorists." [For details see the movie Zeitgeist, part II]. It was clearly staged [an inside job] because:

   a. The *three* buildings fell at virtually free fall speed as only demolition experts have the capability to make them fall.

   b. *Two* airplanes crashing into only *two* buildings could scientifically not possibly have caused any of, let alone, the *three* buildings to fall at this free fall, demolition speed.

   c. There were loads of *molten metal* [steel heated as only demolition "thermite" or "thermate"could scientifically heat it [thermite burns at 4532° F] causing melted iron plus aluminum oxide in the form of astrological amounts of aluminum oxide dust found in a some 2 acre area [87120 square ft area] all around the buildings plus the molten metal (mostly iron)] found in the buildings several weeks after the incident.

   d. *Molten metal* [steel (or iron after the aluminum oxide separates out) melting] requires heat-temperatures much higher, i.e., 2750° Fahrenheit, than the fuel used by airplanes can possibly burn, i.e., 800° F to 1500° F.

   e. This molten metal was found by many experts and other witnesses but not officially reported in any official report.

   f. Cover-ups by the Bush Administration were

obvious [observed] everywhere.

g. Zeitgeist-the movie has quotes connecting a Rockefeller verbally saying beforehand that the event will happen.

h. The list of reasons goes on and on [see Zeitgeist-the movie 122 minutes].

In fact, if 911 weren't a planned pretext, it would be an exception to the rule. The 911 events have been used to provoke two illegal wars. One against Iraq and one against Afghanistan.

It is knowledge in the public domain that the United States has some 200,000 troops stationed all over the world in 144 countries! And at any given time, America usually has 20,000 sailors and Marines deployed afloat on Navy ships. This, in fact, makes America an empire.

Whose empire is it? It is certainly not the empire of the American people! We are told virtually nothing about this empire by our own news media, president or legislators.

It seems to me that it has to be the empire of the international bankers and the large corporations that sprang up around the central bankers as Jefferson warned us about! They are the ones who get virtually all the benefit [profits and loot] from it. They are the ones who are stealing astrological monetary returns at the expense of the American people via this American empire.

I think "big oil" is code for international bankers because the Rothschilds and Rockefellers were originally "big oil" as well as "international bankers" and as far as oil & gas producing wells are concerned, there is no "big oil" in the United States. In 2007 small independent oil & gas operators drilled some 98% of all the oil & gas wells drilled in the United States. Also, in 2007 small independent oil & gas operators owned some 92% of all the oil & gas wells in the United States.

The President, Barack Obama, takes out the public anger against "big oil," i.e., international bankers, on the small independent oil & gas operators of America, and is disastrously trying to tax them out of existence.

However 911 was a pretext for another war as well: The war against you

1. The Patriot Act.
2. Homeland Security.
3. The Military Tribunals Act.
4. Other Legislations were all completely and entirely designed to destroy your civil liberties, i.e., inalienable rights, and limit your ability to fight back against what is coming.
5. Currently, in the United States, unannounced to most brainwashed Americans, your home can be searched without a warrant, without you being home.
6. In turn you can be arrested with no charges revealed to you and detained indefinitely with no access to a lawyer and legally tortured.
7. All under the suspicion that you might be a "Terrorist."
8. If you need a painted picture of what is happening in this country, let's recognized how history repeats itself:

In February 1933, Hitler staged a false flag attack. Burning down his own Parliament Building the Reichstag fire and blamed it on communist "Terrorists."

In the next two weeks he passed the enabling act, which completely eradicated the German Constitution destroying people's liberties and then led to a series of preemptive wars. All justified to the German people as necessary to maintain "Homeland Security:"

"An evil exists that threatens every man, woman, and child of this great nation. We must take steps to secure our domestic security and protect our homeland".—Adolph Hitler

[It looks like it could have been signed by George W. Bush]

This was Hitler's announcement of his Gestapo, [the equivalent of our Homeland Security, CIA or FBI].

"On the matter of communism…and its front organizations should not obscure the issues!"—Adolph Hitler

Reminiscent of Bush saying: *"Our enemies are a network of "Terrorists" and every government that supports them."*

It's time to wake up. The people in power are using the news media as their tool for power and propaganda, go out of their way to make sure you are perpetually mislead and manipulated.

The majority's perception of the world realities is not their own. It is shrewdly imposed upon them without them even knowing it.

For example, the public at large actually believes Iraq is going badly as sectarian violence doesn't seem to stop.

What the public fails to see is that the destabilization of Iraq is exactly what the people behind the government want.

This war is to be maintained so the region can be divided up, domination of the oil, maintained, continual profits reaped for the defense contractors and most importantly permanent military bases established. To be used as a launching pad against other oil bearing non-conforming countries such as Iran and Syria.

For further implication that the destabilizing war is purely intentional: In 2005 two British elite SAS Officers were arrested by Iraqi Police after being caught driving around in their car shooting at civilians while dressed up as Arabs.

After being arrested and taken to a jail in Basra, the British Army immediately requested the release of these men. When the Basra government refused, British Tanks came in and physically broke out the men from the Basra Prison.

If you wish to destroy an area, how do you do it? Two ways:

1. You can go in there and bomb it etc., but that is not very efficient or
2. What you do is you try to get the people in the area to try to kill each other and destroy their own territory.

And that is what was done in that area. The way in which you destroy and burn a country is to get the people to destroy one another by dividing their ranks against one another.

Then you feed both sides. You have agents feeding both sides, inflaming both sides, e.g., our CIA.

It is time that some [or all] of us woke up to this realty. To understand: the people who try to create Empires and maintain them, do it by manipulating the people they are trying to control.

You may want to ask yourself why our entire culture is saturated with mass media entertainment from all sides? Why the education system in America continues its stupefying downward trend?

Why a 71% decline in the education productivity indexes?

The U.S. math rank is 17th and below that of 16 countries:

1. Canada
2. Austria
3. Denmark
4. France
5. Slovak Republic
6. Iceland
7. Germany
8. Sweden
9. Poland
10. Luxembourg
11. Lithuania
12. Norway
13. Hungary
14. Spain

15. Ireland
16. Russia
17. U.S.A.

The U.S. Physics rank is 13th;

1. Denmark
2. Germany
3. Slovenia
4. Australia
5. Cyprus
6. Latvia
7. Greece
8. Swiss
9. Canada
10. France
11. Czech
12. Austria
13. U.S.A.

This all happened since the U.S. Government decided to take over and subsidize our public schools. Why?

We look at government-financed institutions of education and see the kind of students and the kind of education that is being turned out by these government-financed schools.

Logic will tell you that if what is being turned out in those schools was not in accord with the government standards the state and the federal government wanted, then it would change it.

The bottom line is that the government is getting what

they ordered. They do not want your children to be educated.

They do not want you to think too much. That is why our country and our world has become so proliferated with entertainment, mass media, television shows, sports, amusement parks, drugs, alcohol and every kind of entertainment to keep the human mind entertained.

So that you don't get in the way of important people [the master thieves, i.e., the international bankers] by doing too much thinking.

You had better wake up and understand that there are people who are guiding your life and you don't even know it.

Americans have long trended toward reading less and less books and newspapers. Some say that less than 3% of Americans read books, and less than 15% of Americans read News Papers.

More and more, the only "truth" most of us know is what we get over the tube. There are whole and entire generations that don't know anything that didn't come out of the tube.

The actual truth is:

1. America's worst enemies have never been Germany, Russia, North Korea, China, Vietnam, Iraq or Afghanistan.
2. It has been the International Banking Cartels & the large corporations that sprang up around them [as Jefferson warned us about] along with their assistants, i.e., U.S. presidents, senators, representative, judiciary, news media, religion [especially

Christianity], public schools and other stupefying industries, since 1913 when Woodrow Wilson signed the Federal Reserve Act into law.

3. These true enemies of America have sacrificed the lives, liberty, happiness and wealth of honest, stupefied, hard working and conscientious Americans for the banker's & corporations' own pleasure and plunder.

"Let me issue and control a nation's money and I care not who makes its laws."—Mayer Amschel Rothschild [1744-1812], Founder of the Rothschild Dynasty

"When the government fears the people, there is liberty. When the people fear the government, there is tyranny."—Thomas Jefferson

Chapter VI

What Can We Do?

Lately we have been hearing the words "hope" and "faith" a lot. This brings back to mind words in our founding Declaration of Independence: *"Experience hath shewn, that Mankind are more disposed to suffer, while Evils are sufferable, than to right themselves by abolishing the Forms to which they are accustomed."*

Make no mistake; there is a war against the citizens of the United States who are supposed to be the United States itself. We have been loosing that war since 1913, when the international banking cartels established the Federal Reserve Act in the United States.

Our enemies are not who we are told our enemies are!

Our task requires great politicians and as a last resort great military personnel.

I am not a politician nor am I a military man even though I have been in the U.S. Army, put there by the same people who are making us serfdom. I am only an engineer, inventor, artist, writer and entrepreneur.

The job we are confronted with is a job that all Americans have to pitch in to overcome.

All I know is Americans have an extremely important and difficult task in order to survive the attack we are under, which is:

1. To realize there is an extremely serious problem. Then
2. To get rid of our true enemies by legal means if possible: i.e.,
3. The Federal Reserve Cartel along with the corporations that have [as Jefferson told us] sprang up around them of the United States and all ties to the International Banking Cartels, i.e., their assistants with ties to the international banking cartel, such as:
   a. Many key U.S. presidents,
   b. Legislators,
   c. Members of the Judiciary,
   d. Members of the news media, All of a, b, c, and d could well be financed by the International Banking Cartel,
   e. The power of Religion [especially Christianity],
   f. Public schools;
   g. Maybe a private, non-Christian, voucher system is the answer.
   h. And other stupefying industries, brought into existence since 1913 when Woodrow Wilson signed the Federal Reserve Act into law.
4. The really important thing is to get rid of the Federal Reserve System and all ties to the international banking cartel plus we need to get back to the original documents, i.e., the Declaration of Independence, Constitution including the constitutional patent

system and the Bill of Rights.

5. Another thing we must do is get rid of all the beauracracy that have sprang up since the Fed, especially under Roosevelt and get back to the Jeffersonian-Adam Smith [Milton Freedman] economy with no banking Lords in which the government is only a referee and provides the necessary basic functions, e.g.,:

   a. Secure the country from outside invasion.
   b. Assure maximum inalienable rights to each individual in the country
   c. Stop or reduce to the maximum criminal activity.
   d. To thusly make the governmental expense less than 10% of the GDP.

6. If we don't get rid of our true enemies, we will be serfs of the Banking Cartels [Banking Lords] and be basically homeless in the land of our ancestors just like Jefferson, the greatest visionary and friend we ever had, said.

If we only get rid of the Federal Reserve System and all ties to the banking cartels, the rest will probably diminish greatly as a problem and perhaps fall away as a problem, but only if we never let another central bank establish itself in any way.

G. Edward Griffin has organized a largely great organization to overcome the evil now ruling America. Google his name to learn more.

According to Zeitgeist and CNN's Lou Dobbs, the international banking cartel has a much worse agenda! That agenda is *ONE WORLD RULE by The Central Banking Cartel.*

That agenda is already in progress. George Bush secretly signed an agreement to combine the United States, Canada and Mexico into one country, i.e., The North American Union Agreement of 2005.

This one country will be under the rule of the international bankers and will destroy our constitution and founding documents to make us enslaved.

We are to have a new one-world currency: the Amera. We are really in trouble! Make no mistake about it!

Our true enemies want to insert a chip within our bodies wherein the title to all our wealth and everything we own is on this chip and the banking cartels have control of it.

Anytime they choose for any reason they can turn off an individual's chip and eliminate this individual's access to any of his property, which was just stolen by the banking cartels.

Ultimately, we must defeat our true enemies and put back in place the greatest governing documents of all time: the Declaration of Independence, Constitution and Bill of Rights.

Then we must put and keep in place a government that sticks to them and does not have any central bank [or private banking influence] and has a congress that constitionally issues the currency backed by gold.

The money supply should be under the control of a computer program that leads to no injustice whatsoever. No more robberies blamed on free enterprise again.

The congress should eliminate the issuing of money at interest and never use the money supply or credit to oppress, rob and enslave the people. Congress must also truly promote progress in science and the useful arts, i.e., inventions advancing technology.

Congress must keep the laws such that no oppressive organization can ever get out of control in oppressing the people of the United States.

We must avoid anything such as our present day central bank and satellite corporations that can result in a controlling central government as we have today, 2009.

I want to point out that the U.S. Government should, by law, never allow a Bank to get large enough for its leader to do what J.P. Morgan did, and, by law, only Congress should have the power to issue the money as Jefferson said. And every dollar should be backed by gold or real value.

Also, by law, Congress should be required to reimburse or loan to the foreclosed, and thereby enable the foreclosed to pay off the loans so that the Banks could not cause a panic or depression. And runs on banks should be outlawed, e.g., banks should, by law, close after some 15 consecutive withdrawals.

If the foreclosed were loaned the money to pay back the loans foreclosed by the bank Morgan created the run on, Morgan could not create a panic by breaking that bank. When the people regained confidence in the bank and put their money back, the foreclosed barrowers could repay the government by renegotiating with that or another bank for a loan to do so.

Banks should be charged a very stiff fine or jail time if they do deeds that cause a depression or panic. One type of deed would be to purposely make a loan to entities that could not repay the loan to thus bring on panics and depressions. Another type of deed is to allow margin loans that will be described later.

With congress issuing the currency, they should be careful to not issue too much such as was done to bring on the depressions such as we have had at the hand of the Fed.

Therefore, the Bankers could not cause a depression like we have had in our history, i.e., 1907, 1920, 1929, 1938, 1982 and 2009 or overzealous investment such as those which set up the depressions.

It should be clear from this evidence that the red herrings, i.e., Keynesian Economics, Socialism, Communism, Modern Liberalism, are aberrations.

Jeffersonian-Adam Smith [read Milton Freedman's *"Free to Choose"*] economics is as valid as ever. ***It was the Central Bankers who caused the Great Depression.*** The Central Bankers intentionally caused the great depression [*"worked out as we figure a mathematical equation."*] as the beginning step in their enslavement of America.

Printed in the United States
by Baker & Taylor Publisher Services